ISSUE 23, MARCH 2025

AUSTRALIAN FOREIGN AFFAIRS

Contributors

Kim Beazley served as Ambassador of Australia to the United States between 2010 and 2016. A former defence minister, he is currently chair of the Perth USAsia Centre.

James Curran is professor of Modern History at Sydney University and a foreign affairs columnist for the *Australian Financial Review*.

David Heslop is an associate professor at the University of New South Wales and an expert on chemical, biological, radiological and nuclear medicine.

Joe Hockey is a former federal treasurer and served as Ambassador of Australia to the United States between 2016 and 2020.

Joel Keep is a 2024 Biodefense Fellow at the Council on Strategic Risks and a PhD candidate at the University of New South Wales.

Richard McGregor is a senior fellow at the Lowy Institute and worked in China for *The Australian* and the *Financial Times*.

Richard Pomfret is professor of economics emeritus at the University of Adelaide and an adjunct professor at Johns Hopkins University.

Emma Shortis is the director of the International & Security Affairs Program at The Australia Institute.

Arthur Sinodinos is a former federal senator and cabinet minister, and served as Ambassador of Australia to the United States between 2020 and 2023.

Susan Stone is Credit Union SA chair of economics at UniSA.

Thom Woodroofe is a senior international fellow with the Smart Energy Council, and a senior adviser at Kaya Partners.

Australian Foreign Affairs is published three times a year by Australian Foreign Affairs Pty Ltd. Publisher: Morry Schwartz. Editor-in-chief: Erik Jensen. ISBN 978-1-76064-5687 ISSN 2208-5912 Subscriptions: 1-year print and digital subscription (3 issues): $79.00 within Australia incl. GST. 1-year digital-only auto-renew: $49.00. Payment may be made by MasterCard, Visa or Amex, or by cheque made out to Schwartz Books Pty Ltd. Payment includes postage and handling. Subscribe online at www.australianforeignaffairs.com, email subscribe@australianforeignaffairs.com or phone 1800 077 514 / 61 3 9486 0288. Correspondence should be addressed to: The Editor, Australian Foreign Affairs, 22–24 Northumberland Street, Collingwood, VIC, 3066 Australia Phone: 61 3 9486 0288 / Fax: 61 3 9486 0244 Email: enquiries@australianforeignaffairs.com. Editor: Jonathan Pearlman. Deputy Editor: Julian Welch. Associate Editor: Chris Feik. Design: Peter Long. Production Coordination: Marilyn de Castro. Typesetting: Tristan Main. Printed in Australia by McPherson's Printing Group.

Editor's Note

PLANET AUSTRALIA

Donald Trump last visited Australia in 2011, when he promoted *The Apprentice* and delivered addresses to the National Achievers Congress.

In his speech in Sydney, he chided Australia for selling its commodities too cheaply to China ("they need you so badly … screw them"), praised the country's strong economy, entered into some banter with former Miss Universe Jennifer Hawkins, and delivered a series of business lessons that were both embarrassingly vacuous and uncannily prescient ("see yourself as victorious", "get even with people"). Fourteen years later, many of the messages remain familiar – including his criticism of former US president Jimmy Carter for "giving away" the Panama Canal.

There are two significant insights for Australia to be gained from that trip.

First, notwithstanding Trump's friendships with various Australian billionaires and Greg Norman, Australia is a mere blip on the president's global radar. He has no serious business interests here (the New South Wales government rejected his bid to build a casino in the mid-1980s due to his "mafia connections"). In a tweet during his brief 2011 visit, he praised Australia for its "terrific people who love America".

Mostly, Australia's inconsequence is likely to be an advantage during Trump's second presidency. Countries that have a prominent role in his worldview often enter his crosshairs, no matter how close they have been historically to the United States. He wants Canada to become the fifty-first state.

The other significant lesson for Australia is that Trump, a creature of the 1980s, has been strikingly consistent in his main preoccupations. For decades he has called for a return of tariffs, criticised American allies as freeloaders and demanded cuts to the flow of migrants.

Since Trump formed these views, Australia has dramatically changed, as has its place in the world. In the past forty years, US gross domestic product has increased sixfold; Australia's has increased sixteen-fold. Just one Asian country – Japan – was among the world's biggest economies in 1985; now there are three: China, Japan and India. It is not just Australia but much of the world that now looks to find its security and prosperity in Asia.

The challenge for Australia will be to try to secure its opportunities in Asia, including its soaring trade with China, even as Trump risks undermining them.

Too often Trump's erratic nature has led to a focus in Australia on whether he will undermine the US–Australia alliance. But much of this fretting is unwarranted. Australia, if anything, has become more militarily important to the United States, and has already started sending hundreds of millions of dollars to Washington as part of the AUKUS deal.

The challenges that Trump poses are deeper and more difficult than whether he will grant Australia's prime minister another US state dinner. Trump's interests are elsewhere. There will be no Asia pivot.

Australia needs to understand how Trump's America works and how a superpower works when it has global interests but is avowedly self-centred. This is a new and unsettling dilemma for Australia. We need to consider our response.

In 2011 Trump offered a solution of his own: "You have to see yourself as a one-man band," he told the National Achievers Congress. "Don't rely too much on other people because they'll let you down."

Jonathan Pearlman

CONTINENTAL GIFT

Trump and Australia's place in the world

James Curran

History will little remember how, following the US election in November 2024, the usual suspects attempted to round up the Australian public and sow fear about what Donald Trump might do. The questions being asked betrayed an extraordinary lack of confidence in the American alliance, at sharp remove from the rhetoric of it as "unbreakable": whether Trump might take a set against Prime Minister Anthony Albanese or shun his Labor predecessor Kevin Rudd, now Australia's ambassador in Washington, and whether he might look sceptically on AUKUS, ask for a greater Australian financial contribution to the US submarine industrial base or target Canberra with tariffs. Inventories were compiled of which Australian policies might gel or jar with those of the incoming administration. It has been a foolish and futile exercise.

So panicked were some pundits that they demanded Albanese rush to Florida or Washington for an early meeting with the president-elect.

The prime minister inadvertently gave voice to the same kinds of underlying anxieties when he repeated in media interviews Trump's remark during their initial telephone conversation: that the two countries would enjoy a "perfect friendship". It revealed the deep-seated Australian desire to be liked, the phrase becoming a virtual life raft to which the country could cling in the coming Trumpian storm. But it is a fair bet Albanese was not the only leader around the world who received the promise.

The unease is also surprising, given how well placed Australia is for Trump's return to office. The predicament arises from two main sources. The first is that Trump's second term, much like the first, will be almost solely concerned with how Washington manages relations with great powers, particularly China, Russia, India and Europe. As the former British head of MI6 John Sawers observed, these states will dominate Trump's chessboard: "powers to be contained, beaten and played off against each other in a zero-sum logic". Trump's focus, at least during the first few months in office, will be on what he can get the Europeans to do in shoring up Ukraine's security as the war is brought to a close, probably via a negotiated settlement that freezes the conflict. Trump may demand that Russia apply pressure on Iran to back off Israel. Australia can have little say or effect on the policy outcomes in either of these theatres.

The second relates to just how fully Australia, by virtue of its fiscal contribution to the US nuclear-powered submarine industry and the growing American military presence in the country, already satisfies

Trump's transactional impulse when it comes to alliances. This follows a profound shift over the past quarter-century in how Australia manages relations with Washington. The policy of "alliance maintenance" adopted by successive governments in Canberra involves giving the United States more and more access to Australian military facilities and territory. The consequence is that Australia is now locked into US strategy for Asia, which is to contest and contain China's rise. Officials in Canberra are loath to admit this publicly, but during a visit last August, the chair of the US House of Representatives Foreign Affairs Committee, Michael McCaul, presented a more direct expression of the reality. Australia, he said, is now "the central base of the Indo-Pacific to counter the [China] threat".

In essence, this represents Australia's continental gift to the United States, comprising marine rotations, airfields and logistics hubs, not to mention a new base for US nuclear-powered submarines on the coast of Western Australia. This diplomatic and geopolitical bequest is surely set to render much of the post-election panic moot.

An Americanist, not a globalist

For allies such as Australia, the manual on how to handle Trump from his first term in office is of virtually no use. Then, Canberra's response was threefold: appeal to Washington to rediscover its belief in the international order it shaped after World War II, educate President Trump in the value of alliances and invoke basic economic common sense in securing a reprieve from Trump's steel and aluminium tariffs.

The appeal to American altruism largely fell on deaf ears, but the history lesson about military "mateship" served its purpose, for a time, and Australia escaped the tariffs. But generally, Australian policymakers did not want to believe that Trump might be bringing the Pax Americana to a close.

Trump's election triumph in late 2024 means that his first term can no longer be dismissed as an aberration. Coming on top of September 11, the damage to American credibility caused by the Iraq War and the global financial crisis, Trump's election in 2016 delivered another shock to traditional ideas of American power and purpose. His return does not signal an American retreat from the world, even if the American middle class continues to reject a more ambitious foreign policy. Rather, it likely foreshadows a president even more determined to get his way on the world stage, and with fewer voices of caution and restraint around him. Trump's comments before and since his inauguration about possible US intervention in Panama, Greenland and Canada give voice to a new style of American empire. This is not neoconservative-style "democracy promotion" at the point of a rifle, but it is about wielding imperial power carelessly and certainly unsubtly. Its message can be simply summarised: get out of America's way.

The manual on how to handle Trump from his first term in office is of virtually no use

This message, and Trump's blizzard of announcements once he took office, not to mention the thread of virtual submission and acceptance to his will around the world as it took place, also demonstrates a phenomenon not well understood until now. Namely, that the United States' long-enduring "soft power", fashioned by American popular culture, has been hijacked almost overnight by Trump to touch a nerve of conservative, and notably male, reaction around the world. And, as far as we can gauge, in the suburbs and regions of Australia. As a result, Trump's caudillo style of presidency is now the most prominent part of a continuum alongside Facebook and Instagram, a popular culture that is the environment of mass attention.

Perhaps the best descriptor, which should be imprinted on the minds of policymakers and strategists the world over, is the one allegedly said by a first-term Trump staffer: "Globalism means to sacrifice the nation to save the empire. 'America first' means to sacrifice the empire to save the nation." What Donald Trump wants to revive most of all is the American "dream". The kind of country that Irish poet Seamus Heaney once described as "like an immense hovercraft, buoyant on its own prosperity and trust in the future". Speaking about America in the 1980s, Heaney said it was as if they had "lived for years in a geodesic dome of continental proportions – communally, sumptuously insulated from the cold blast of world poverty, not prone to anxiety about dangers in the civic and political realm", inside a "centrally heated" dream.

That's not to indulge in the myth of a golden age of American reach and influence. Even when US power was at its height between 1945 and

1991, it could not stop the triumph of Mao's communists in China in 1949, an event that became known as the "loss of China", haunting America's East Asia policy until Nixon broke the ice with Peking in 1972. Washington also failed to stop the rise of Fidel Castro in Cuba in 1959 and the Shia revolution in Iran in 1979. In South Vietnam, in the name of shoring up US credibility and convinced of falling dominoes, the Americans failed to ask basic questions about whether the local conditions were ripe for the kind of democracy they wished to instil. These same questions were not sufficiently posed before the invasion of Iraq in 2003.

America's ongoing advantages must, however, give pause to the prophets of decline. The United States still leads in technology and AI, though the recent Chinese announcement on DeepSeek has badly rattled American confidence. Its economy remains the largest in terms of nominal GDP: in the third quarter of 2024 its GDP increased by 3.1 per cent. It is energy-independent for the first time since the OPEC crisis of the early 1970s and its population continues to grow. Much of this is due not only to demographics but to immigration: even Trump says that a healthy, legal migrant intake is the quid pro quo of tougher crackdowns on illegal entrants.

Trump's China riddle

Trump, like any president, will pursue personal, political and national interests. Allies can bet that the personal takes priority. His cabinet picks are a collective lacking in a common character. It remains to be seen whether Trump's relationship with Elon Musk can survive differences over trade policy with China, and whether the China hawks such as Marco Rubio as Secretary of State and Mike Waltz as National Security Advisor can infuse Trump and Vance's policy towards Beijing with a more confrontational, ideological edge. That would be some transformation. In his nomination hearing before the US Congress, Rubio said China had "lied, cheated, hacked and stolen their way to global superpower status, at our expense". In those fourteen words he gave voice to so much of the hurt and betrayal felt by American political elites at China's rise. Further decoded, what Rubio was really saying was that history was not meant to turn out like this.

Consider too the significant changes Trump faces since leaving office in January 2021: the decline of Iranian power and influence, Israel's independence of Washington, the question of what replaces the Assad regime in Damascus, the new conditions Saudi Arabia has placed on Palestine for an accord with Israel, and the damage to American credibility in the region arising from its withdrawal from Afghanistan, an exit that left much of Central Asia exposed to Islamist fundamentalist terror. Ukraine confronts manpower and resources shortages. The far right is on the rise in Eastern Europe, Italy and France. Germany is in a political muddle, with strong pro-Putin forces in its east and declining commitment to Kyiv in Berlin. China's economy is stressed, while North Korea has sent troops to Ukraine to gain combat experience. The BRICS alliance – whose ten members include Brazil, China, India, Iran, Indonesia, Russia, and South Africa – has a new significance, and, with the exception of the Philippines, ASEAN neutrality is becoming more decisive. New Indonesian president Prabowo's first overseas trip after winning the February 2024 elections was to Beijing; his first trip after inauguration in October was to the same place.

Trump and Vance want military strength so that they don't have to worry about the outside world, but the risk is that sometimes you get into a war without looking for it. Trump believes he can pull off a great, Metternich-style breakthrough on China and perhaps the Korean Peninsula too – but he won't be remembered as a great leader if the cost of living goes up further in the United States, which is what his tariff policy is likely to do.

> **Trump believes he can pull off a great, Metternich-style breakthrough on China**

Trump's nomination of Rubio and Waltz presents something of a riddle to those trying to divine Washington's China policy over the next four years. Trump and Vance are on record saying they do not want a military confrontation with China. Trump, as before, neither invokes the ideological fervour of American nationalism nor speaks of China as an "existential threat" to American primacy. And both he and Vance have excoriated the Washington foreign policy establishment for the "forever" wars in the Middle East.

So Trump could well be playing with Chinese minds already. Going into November, he spoke of his plan for a "surprise" when it came to Beijing but would not reveal his negotiating strategy. But will Congress let him go down this path if it means any diminution of US support for

Taiwan? It is unlikely. Trump told *The Wall Street Journal* he "wouldn't have to" use military force against China in the event it moved on Taiwan, because Xi Jinping "respects me, and he knows I'm f—ing crazy". Trump's answer to any such move would be to impose tariffs "at 150 per cent to 200 per cent" on China, or shut down trade altogether.

Evan Medeiros, Barack Obama's China consigliere, wrote in the *Financial Times* in November 2024 that "there are credible scenarios for both a big deal, a grand bargain on economic or security issues, or a big fall, as relations deteriorate into a deep freeze or even military confrontation". Trump's China policy will likely be once more centred on trade and industrial policy, a point of agreement between Republicans and Democrats. It remains to be seen what Trump and Vance make of the "high fence, small yard" strategy left to them by President Joe Biden and National Security Advisor Jake Sullivan, but they will hardly abandon the task of reshoring manufacturing. The internal conflict over policy may come if Musk and the Silicon Valley tech world feel their priorities on China slip to second place in the administration's thinking.

The gifting of a continent

The first briefing Trump receives on Australia will surely underline just how significant Australia has become to US warfighting in the Asia-Pacific and to the broader American strategic posture in Asia. This arguably has its origins in the Global Force Posture Review commenced during the George W. Bush administration. But its pace and import have quickened dramatically in the last decade. Indeed, defence planners in the Pentagon now divide their strategic map of the Australian continent into three distinct, though interconnected, segments.

The Pentagon's first zone is the north of Australia, primarily – in Washington's eye – the site for US "force projection". Here, Darwin, involving the rotating presence of 2000 US marines on six-month deployments, and the stationing of US aircraft, including, eventually, B-52 bombers at RAAF Base Tindal, near Katherine, is central. This would also include the coming upgrades to airfields across northern Queensland, the Northern Territory and Western Australia, at RAAF Bases Scherger, Curtin and Learmonth. The intelligence facilities at Pine Gap and North West Cape, so central to US war planning and the defence of the United States itself, are also critical.

In the middle of the country, the Americans see the potential for a number of logistics hubs.

Southern Australia, stretching from the New South Wales–Victoria border across to Perth, is the "soft underbelly", as some in the Pentagon apparently refer to it. This is for industrial production, comprising the major population centres such as Melbourne, Perth and Adelaide that will support planned AUKUS submarine, frigate and munitions manufacture.

It has, of course, long been known how critical Australia's strategic geography is for American warfighting and deterrence of China. This planned integration was laid out in the US–Australian agreements of 2011, on US marines in Darwin, and in 2014, on force posture.

But informed discussion of these significant details of our increasingly intimate alliance is non-existent. There has been no serious public or political debate in Australia about whether providing offensive capability to the United States is something to which the country should agree, or about how the risks compare to those which, since the Cold War, have stemmed from Australia's hosting of the joint intelligence facilities.

These are serious questions. While force projection clearly motivates American thinking, is there any consideration of these facilities being a target for China, and of how they are protected? Does the stationing of US B-52 bombers at Tindal, for example, increase Australia's vulnerability to attack, or does it increase the likelihood of US protection?

Regardless, does Australia want such involvement in a shooting war when it might not have any say in the fighting of that war? Or did Pine Gap effectively answer that question years ago? Have these thoughts crossed the mind of the defence minister and the national security committee of cabinet? Unless the public is advised otherwise, the assumption must be no. There is, after all, no national security reason to not discuss these issues with the Australian people. The United States finds no difficulty in ventilating the realities of their Australian force projection.

Australia's prominence in US war planning is now a critical part of a near decade-long project to disperse US military assets across the region. Washington is repurposing a series of World War II–era airfields and installations in the Western Pacific so that it has the capacity to move aircraft quickly away from their major military hubs at Kadena Air Base, in Okinawa, and Andersen Air Force Base, on Guam. US access to a greater number of airfields in the Philippines operates on the same principle.

This "scatter and survive" policy compliments the "latticework" system of alliances and partnerships in Asia that the United States has structured since late last century. The struts of the latticework crisscross much of East Asia. But US military policy is also stretching further south, away from the first and second island chain and towards Australia. That's primarily about reducing the vulnerability to US planes and ships now concentrated in Okinawa and Guam, making the targeting of US assets more difficult in a conflict in the Taiwan Strait.

Fear of China and fealty to the US alliance are now fused

All this plays into powerful memories of the American military presence in Australia during World War II. The difference, of course, is the Japanese attack on Pearl Harbor in December 1941, which brought the United States into the war, and with it the decision to come in strength to Australia. But Australia is now involved in contingency planning for a war of undefined provocation or cause. A bigger US footprint here does not necessarily equate to a greater say in the making of policy, or access to the innermost American war councils. Just ask Kevin Rudd, who arrived in Washington as ambassador expecting to become a standing member of the National Security Council when it discussed China. He did not make it to the front door.

But there is something about today that is reminiscent of the situation during World War II, best summed up by US General Douglas Macarthur's comment to his British liaison officer in October 1942: that when he'd arrived from the Philippines earlier that year, "Curtin and Co. more or less offered him the country on a platter". If there is a historical analogy to be drawn, it is surely the words of the then American minister in Canberra: the Australian "seeming to expect us to do everything for him, fight for him and work for him". An Australian, he judged, was a creature incapable of "seeing beyond his surfing beaches". US policy planners may well have assessed that Australia's best contribution to any future war effort is as it was in 1941: the full and unimpeded resources of the Australian continent, rather than any genuine contribution at the frontline.

Interests and culture

This continental gift represents a decisive marker in the history of Australia's relations with the world. Up until, say, the mid to late 1990s, there remained a creative tension in Australian foreign and defence policy, between the pull of history and the imperative of geography, between Canberra's cultural attachments to its great-power protectors and the recognition that it had distinctive interests arising from its geopolitical position on the edge of Asia.

That dynamic meant that the task of Australian policymakers from before World War I was to align these cultural loyalties with Australia's distinctive political interests, to make London and Washington see

Australia's Pacific concerns as commensurate with their own. In short, to ensure that its protectors saw the defence of Australia as integral to their own defence. But these efforts proved a mirage: policymakers in Canberra found on more than one occasion that the great powers tended to play fast and loose with Australian interests: that the United States and United Kingdom would prioritise other theatres of conflict over their own, as was the case in the initial stages of World War II, or that they would fail to consult Canberra on matters directly affecting Australia, or that Australian leaders and officials would be excluded from the senior councils where American and British policy towards the region was being formed. Australian feelings of "betrayal" over the failure of the Singapore strategy in 1942, its exclusion from crucial Allied conferences in Cairo and Tehran where plans for the post-war Pacific were discussed, and the failure of Curtin's efforts to revive imperial defence in 1944 all exemplify this despair at not being able to have the kind of influence in Britain and the United States they felt was deserved. Chifley and Evatt then tried on no less than three occasions in the late 1940s to get Washington to agree to some kind of Pacific pact or presidential statement of support for Australia, but they failed each time. And external affairs minister Percy Spender, though signing off on the ANZUS Treaty, lamented that it did not give Canberra access to US global strategic planning.

These experiences and painful wartime memories led Australian governments during the Cold War to intensify their efforts in enjoining London and Washington in Australia's defence, especially in South-East Asia. For a time this was achieved, as Australia fought alongside Britain in the Malayan insurgency and supported America in Vietnam. The two sides of Australian policy had come together. But in matters more directly affecting Australian security, especially related to Indonesia, Australia found that its interests and those of its great-power protector – in that case America – diverged. In a remark that should still haunt Australian policymakers, President John F. Kennedy told Australian external affairs minister Garfield Barwick in October 1963 that the American people had "forgotten ANZUS" and that therefore Canberra should not count on US military support if it got into direct conflict with Indonesia during the Confrontation crisis of the early 1960s.

Then, with Britain's retreat from Asia and formal entry into Europe, and with the recalibration of America's position in Asia following defeat in Vietnam, Australia was forced, despite itself, to reassess its foreign and defence policy. Australia understood that it had to pursue its own interests in making a new home for itself in Asia. Asia was freed from Western domination, and Australia was shedding its "White Australia" skin. Continental defence was adopted. And while the effort to find a place in Asia started tentatively under Holt and Gorton, it was given its most dramatic flourish under the Whitlam, Fraser and, later, Hawke and Keating governments. In short, while recognising the ongoing importance of the US alliance to Australia's defence, those governments prioritised engagement with the region over the older cultural loyalties. They understood that Australia would have to make its own way in Asia and find new acceptance in the region.

But this lodestar of Australian policy, the tension between culture and interest, has now reached something of a resolution. It can be read two ways: first, that with the recognition by the United States that Australia constitutes its key launching pad for a China containment policy, Canberra policymakers have now achieved a longstanding aim to ensure that the Americans see the defence of Australia as integral to the defence of the United States.

Second, it might also be seen as Australia aligning its community of culture – that is, its loyalty to the United States – with its community of interest, the distinctive factors that arise from Australia's place in the world. Fear of China and fealty to the alliance are now fused in a way unlike any other period in Australian history. Australia assumes that the two are being brought into alignment: that culture and interest are mutually reinforcing in a policy of "alliance maintenance", and that loyalty to Washington, giving the United States more and more, equates to a guaranteed defence of Australian interests. The assumptions here, however, are many, including the assumption that a war over Taiwan that could quickly turn nuclear and devastate East Asia is in Australia's interests.

Australia assumes that loyalty to Washington equates to a guaranteed defence of Australian interests

So how has this point been reached?

Explaining this new circumstance requires an understanding of how culture and identity have shaped the trajectory of Australian foreign and defence policy. Arguably, the starting point was in 1996. At the federal election that year, the slogan of the Howard Opposition was that its foreign policy would be "Asia first but not Asia only". Indeed, in one of the supporting documents on a Coalition government's approach to the world, Asia was referred to as the "East". It was an unfortunate slip.

This is not to say that the Howard government ignored Asia during the succeeding terms. Its record on the Asian Financial Crisis, its intervention in East Timor in 1999, the signing of the Lombok Treaty, its securing of membership of the East Asia Summit and its signing of free trade agreements with a number of partners refute the idea that Australia somehow went missing in the region. But what lingers, still, is the perception of Australia as the "deputy sheriff", and the remarkable comment from John Howard that he would sanction a pre-emptive strike on a regional country if there was evidence it had weapons of mass destruction.

Culturally, the Howard period was also deeply significant. From the 1970s Australia had searched in vain for a post-imperial successor myth, a way of defining the country that was as powerful as British race patriotism had been from the late 19th century down to the 1960s. The bush legend, the Eureka Stockade, Gallipoli, even the "Bodyline" cricket series: all were given a go. And all failed to muster much popular enthusiasm or give Australia a self-sufficient nationalism. Nevertheless, from the election of Whitlam to the end of the Keating government, there was broad agreement that Australia was pursuing engagement with Asia, that its formal constitutional links with Britain were declining and that it was seeking to come to terms with its poor record on the treatment of the nation's Indigenous peoples.

Howard rejected the idea of national "navel gazing" and defined Australia through the prism of the Anzac legend. Around it was also wrapped a rhetoric – and Howard again was the first to do this – that divined an Australian military tradition stretching all the way from Baghdad in 2003 to the colonial contingents that served with General Gordon in the Sudan in 1885. Further, over the next two decades, the commemorative culture of Anzac became indistinguishable from ennobling the US alliance in Australian history. The slouch hat became folded into the nation's strategic doctrine. "One hundred years of mateship" with America, according to former prime minister Scott Morrison, was going to lead to "one hundred more".

All of this became a bipartisan enterprise. Labor, scorched by the episode of Mark Latham's leadership in 2004, in which its alliance credentials were as seriously questioned as they had been during the Cold War, became ever more determined to prove its American loyalties. The party's left wing, largely eviscerated in the 1980s debates over the joint intelligence facilities, shrivelled further to the point of virtual disappearance. So Kevin Rudd got dewy-eyed seeing John Curtin's name in the Blair House visitor's notebook when he first visited Washington as prime minister, and informally saluted President George W. Bush at the NATO summit in Bucharest; Julia Gillard told a joint sitting of the US Congress that she'd grown up with an America "that could do anything". The path to Australia being locked into American grand strategy in Asia, through Obama's "pivot" speech to the Commonwealth parliament in 2011, the force posture changes signed by Tony Abbott and Julie Bishop in 2014 or AUKUS under Scott Morrison, followed a singular direction: into the American embrace. How, then, could President Biden's deputy secretary of state, Kurt Campbell, have thought AUKUS was necessary to get Australia "off the fence"?

Closing the eyes

Trump is unlikely to turn on Australia. But the counterfactual might actually be worth exploring: if Trump turns on us, it might force Canberra to think about what there is to Australian foreign policy other than the US alliance.

Equally, aspects of Trump's international policy, particularly on Gaza, climate and trade, may not sit well with the Australian electorate. That could make it difficult for Australian governments to fall back on the deepening integration of Australian and US military force postures, complicating the domestic management of support for the alliance. The personality of the American president has rarely, if ever, caused a precipitous decline in public support for the US relationship, but the unpredictability of Trump is a factor all its own. The point, then, is not that America is in decline, but that the America to which Australia has become accustomed is changing.

Consider, though, the bottom line with the current debate over the AUKUS agreement, especially its Pillar 1 component: to deliver

Australia a nuclear-powered submarine capability. Even with doubts about its realisation, it has been taken by many to be acceptable because it means building bridges with the United States. Some of the most pro-alliance officials and ex-officials must surely know, in their heart of hearts, that AUKUS will be a Potemkin. Yet neither the myriad challenges facing British and American shipyards nor the difficulty of Australia developing a nuclear submarine industry appear to dent the public projection of confidence in the project. That's because AUKUS is primarily about building a deeper strategic alignment with America. And that, in turn, stems from the belief that the Chinese are intrinsic hegemons who will exercise military predominance in Asia. This Australian view arises not from racism but from fear. But the same group that accepts an illusory AUKUS does not appear to grasp that, given China's economic heft, Beijing will likely exercise that kind of hegemony over Australia anyway.

So the bases have been given over to Washington. Whenever Prime Minister Albanese meets President Trump, he will say all the right things and smile for the cameras at all the right times. He, or perhaps his successor Peter Dutton – I am writing this in early February – will arrive in Washington laden with yet more strategic gifts for the White House. Others in Canberra will simply close their eyes to Trump, hoping to find something more familiar when they awaken four years later. ■

DADDY ISSUES

Finding ourselves in Trump world

Emma Shortis

Twenty days after his election victory was confirmed, Donald Trump issued a decree on his social media platform, Truth Social. On his first day in office, he promised, he would "sign all necessary documents to charge Mexico and Canada a 25% Tariff on ALL products coming into the United States".

A blanket tariff would, of course, be disastrous for the Canadian economy. Dealing with inter-provincial tensions at home, and confronting the perils of incumbency, the Canadian prime minister, Justin Trudeau, scrambled to respond. He spoke to Trump on the phone and, a few days later, flew to Florida to dine at Mar-a-Lago with the president-elect.

Trudeau met with "Judge" Jeanine Pirro and Trump's (second) choice for attorney-general, Pam Bondi. He was granted a spot at the top table with Trump, alongside some of his cabinet picks. As usual, Trump played iPad DJ with his whiplash-inducing song choices. "On at least one occasion," the *Canadian Globe and Mail* noted, "Mr. Trump paused the conversation to point out a high note that [Luciano] Pavarotti was about to hit." At another point, Trump "joked" with Trudeau about making Canada the fifty-first state of the United States. It was, Trump later said, a "very productive" evening.

Trudeau posted about the evening too, including a photo: his unfussy complexion, hair and suit presented a stark contrast to the weirdly bronzed skin, bright veneers and too-long tie of the former and now future so-called leader of the so-called free world. Trudeau's post was anodyne, a blank slate on which any intention could be projected: "Thanks for dinner last night, President Trump. I look forward to the work we can do together, again."

But in Trudeau's photo the two men are sitting a little too close. Trudeau's smile is too big, too forcefully normal. He is, quite clearly, only a visitor, a northern imposter in this southern enclave of power, admitted only at the whim of the president-elect, which might change at any moment, without warning. And, despite his very best efforts, Prime Minister Trudeau left Florida, as the *Guardian* reported, "without any assurances".

Responses in Canada were mixed. One report in the *Globe and Mail* described the night as "one of the most important dinner dates Justin Trudeau has ever secured". Another possible interpretation was that Trudeau, the consummate establishment liberal, left Florida if not humiliated, then at least put firmly in his place. Not long after the dinner, Trump posted about tariffs again, this time with a nod to "Governor Justin Trudeau of the Great State of Canada".

The Canadian PM was the first of the G7 leaders to meet with Trump since his election victory. More followed. They're all justifiably worried – about Trump, and about their own political futures. They should be.

Not long after his encounter with Trump, Trudeau announced his resignation. He leaves a Liberal Party in disarray, with little prospect of turning its fortunes around before the next election. Trump supporters gleefully claimed Trudeau as their first scalp. They are confident there will be more. Trump's (far) right-hand man, Elon Musk, is actively supporting radical, white supremacist movements in both the United Kingdom and Germany, and is likely to expand his efforts as his confidence grows.

Trudeau's cycle of humiliation and desperation will be repeated, again and again and again.

The desperate scramble

The world was not ready for Trump's return.

Some governments, Hungary and Israel among them, keenly anticipated his election victory. But most democratic governments were apprehensive, torn between belief and hope that a Trump victory would not happen. As a result, they had not adequately prepared for what he would do. They were left, once again, desperately scrambling to win his favour.

In media coverage and analysis outside the United States, including in Australia, much of the focus on that scrambling looks not at the actual consequences of the constant competition for favour but at how effective that scrambling might be, relative to the scrambling of other competitors.

As one high-profile foreign policy figure in Australia noted not long after the election, in apparently deep concern: President Emmanuel Macron of France, despite a rocky history with Trump, had managed to persuade him to attend the highly symbolic reopening of Notre-Dame cathedral in Paris in December, more than a month before his inauguration. British Labour prime minister Keir Starmer was quick to assure the Americans he would seek "closer" security ties. The secretary-general of NATO visited Trump at Mar-a-Lago soon after the election, a few days before Trudeau got there. "Everyone," this commentator continued, "is making moves. What's ours?"

What will it say about us if Trump does, in fact, like us?

The international response to Trump – including here in Australia, as this question so forcefully conveys – appears to be motivated by a narrow set of questions that reflect an even narrower set of interests. Among them: what can we give him? What can we offer Trump to keep him onside, to placate him? How can we convince him that we're good, that he needs us, that it's not *us* he should punish? *What are our moves?*

Writing in *The London Review of Books*, Tom Stevenson observed, very Britishly, "In Britain, one might expect Trump's impending return to provoke some questioning of the extent the country has tied itself to the US." Stevenson's understatement emphasises the excruciating irony of the situation in which America's NATO and ANZUS partners now find themselves. The same questions must be asked by Canadians, by the other members of NATO, by South Korea, by Japan and by Australia.

Alas, that is not happening. In the United Kingdom, the chair of the House of Commons' Business and Trade Committee, Liam Byrne, instead suggested, in Stevenson's words, "that Britain should bargain with Trump for an exemption from the tariffs by offering to move even further towards the US position on China".

It is a pattern being repeated by leaders the world over, who are all scrambling for essentially the same thing: continued American benevolence in return for their subservience. They are scrambling to convince Trump that they matter, that he shouldn't hurt them, because doing so would also hurt America. They are desperately trying to find the right way to lay out the facts, to put the words in an order that he can understand, as if that matters. The unspoken problem is, of course, that not everyone can get a carve-out. That's not how it works. If everyone gets an exemption, then no one is punished – and that is not Trump's style, and hardly a path he's likely to take. So Trump is able to hold these threats over the rest of the world's figurative heads, doling out the occasional favour, sometimes deigning to let them dine with him in the tacky surrounds of his Florida palace. Meanwhile, the rest of the world are fighting among themselves for the scraps of his benevolence.

As Trump drily observed to NBC's Kristen Welker in his first mainstream sit-down interview after the election, "People like me now, you know?" He likes the scrambling. It looks like winning.

And so far, it is. Trump fractures everything. Only this time around, it's worse. And allowing it to happen again is much less forgivable.

But the pressure to fall back on the patterns of the first Trump administration is immense. In Australia, driven largely by the Murdoch media outlets, this takes the form of asking whether Kevin Rudd should continue as ambassador, given that Trump doesn't like him and he doesn't even play golf. This view uncritically accepts that, during Trump's first term, Ambassador Joe Hockey's tactic of golfing with the president is what saved us from disaster. (No matter that, as Malcolm Turnbull has pointed out, Hockey did not play *with* him so much as *near* him, and only once or twice, with Greg Norman as midwife.) The inevitable conclusion of such logic is that a Labor government should appoint an arch-conservative former Liberal prime minister as some kind of special envoy to the president, as if that would be either ideologically reconcilable or in the current government's interests.

To use the language of Trump world, all this handwringing can be distilled down into one big, whining question: how do we make sure Daddy stays?

Most analysis assumes that the Australian government will inevitably have to play this game of courting Trump again, of *making our moves* – but that this time it will be harder, because he probably won't like the current prime minister as much as he liked the last one. That is, almost universally, assumed to be a bad thing. This mindset tends to preclude the obvious answer: that Daddy is toxic, and abusive, and we might be safer and better off if he *doesn't* stay.

Because none of this handwringing and self-flagellation deals with what it will look like to stay close to Trump's version of America – what it will mean for Australia's security and future. What will it say about us if Trump does, in fact, like us?

It's easy to imagine Albanese meeting with Trump – the awkward, stilted conversation and photos, the forced laughter, the prime minister trying desperately to appear at ease. The excruciating nods to "common values" with a man who has staffed his administration with white supremacists, misogynists and Christian nationalists, who has threatened, repeatedly, to use the military against his own people, and whose radical agenda will break what little is left of the international rule of law and may well plunge the global economy into deep recession and lock in catastrophic global warming.

Such an approach by Albanese is widely assumed to be entirely appropriate and obviously necessary. Sometimes, as Phil Coorey wrote in the *Australian Financial Review* long before Trump's victory, "cosying up to a madman" is "a necessity".

But is it? Why?

Working with monsters

Even before Trump's cataclysmic election win, it was a truism to say that a second Trump administration would be much scarier than the first. But it is the truth. There will be echoes of his first go around, such as in the high rate of staff turnover, which began mere days after his election victory in November. But the constant parade of incompetent TV stars will – perhaps deliberately – obscure the machinations of their more competent underlings.

The fanatical ideologues Trump has tapped to run his administration see themselves as the guardians of a generational project of the American right. Their victory in November 2024 has handed them the most powerful executive since that of Franklin D. Roosevelt, plus the House and Senate, and has cemented what will now be a decades-long Republican hold on the Supreme Court. They will not waste this opportunity. And they will not give it up willingly. They – like Trump – have no interest in democracy. They are interested, instead, in maintaining minority rule and implementing a particularly American brand of fascism.

How, exactly, should the Australian attorney-general work with such people?

At issue here is Trump's imperative to breathe new life into the oligarchic neoliberalism that has divided America and brought it to the point that it cannot protect itself from itself. Trump embodies the tendency to self-destruction that Nick Bryant has so terrifyingly portrayed in *The Forever War*.

Dealing with a Trump administration means dealing with more than just an autocratic and unpredictable president. Conversations and meetings with Trump himself are relatively rare – the Australian prime minister will likely get only a few of them. The real work of the relationship happens below the level of heads of state: between ministers and secretaries, and via the exchanges between their departments.

Even thinking through the practicalities of that should be alarming. To take one example: during his visits to the United States before the election, Australian attorney-general Mark Dreyfus held discussions about cooperation in law enforcement, meeting with senior figures in the Biden administration such as White House deputy chief of staff Bruce Reed and the secretary of the Department of Homeland Security, Alejandro Mayorkas. If the attorney-general were to repeat such visits now, he would likely be meeting with Stephen Miller and Kristi Noem.

Miller, a fixture in Trump world, could be generously described as a white nationalist. He will oversee Trump's plan to implement the largest mass deportations in American history. In 2018, in the midst of the family separations crisis, one White House adviser told *Vanity Fair* that Miller was "a twisted guy... he's Waffen-SS". In the intervening six years, Miller's views appear only to have hardened.

Kirsti Noem, a former governor of South Dakota who has no law-enforcement experience, will likely be manipulated and overruled by Miller and Tom Homan, a hardliner whom Trump has tapped to run Immigration and Customs Enforcement. But Noem shares their views: when she's not killing her own pets or lying about meeting North Korean dictator Kim Jong-un, she uses Trump's fascist rhetoric about an immigrant "invasion".

How, exactly, should the Australian attorney-general work with such people without compromising the values and interests of his government? How can he possibly make nice with Miller and Noem – not to mention others, such as Trump's pick as Director of National Intelligence, Tulsi Gabbard, or FBI head Kash Patel?

To take another, perhaps more obvious, example: Australia's Minister for Foreign Affairs, Penny Wong, will have to make nice with an administration that is actively opposed to her, and her family's, ability to exist safely in public. Wong would represent, to them, the epitome of the "diversity, equity and inclusion" candidate, easily dismissed and actively denigrated. Wong will be dealing with an administration that is actively and enthusiastically harming women and LGBTIQA+ people at home and abroad. This is not to denigrate Wong's diplomatic ability, which is considerable – as foreign minister, she deals regularly with counterparts who have clashing values and interests. It is to note that the current framework of Australian foreign policy and the US alliance requires that the foreign minister actively seek out deeper cooperation with even this American administration, and that she talk of "common values" with people who hate her and all that she represents. In the process, they will attempt to force Wong to debase herself and, by extension, the country.

And for what?

All this is assumed to be a "necessity", as Phil Coorey insisted, for Australia's security. Despite Trump, despite all that he represents and will do, the Australian government must "make moves" to preserve the security alliance and the AUKUS submarine pact. They must save us from the worst excesses of Trump *and* keep him from abandoning us.

What kind of "security" is that, really? What kind of world will it create?

War and machismo

The world Trump inherits is already full of danger and despair. Politicians and self-proclaimed foreign policy pundits claim that we now face "the worst strategic circumstances since World War II" and – often simultaneously – a "new Cold War". That isn't how history works, and both are lazy comparisons, but they are sticky – for understandable reasons.

President Joe Biden prided himself on his foreign policy experience, but he oversaw a dramatic deterioration in global stability. His administration's approach to Russia's invasion of Ukraine has repeated many of the mistakes of America's past, focusing not on the difficult negotiations required for genuine peacebuilding but on weapons supply. His blanket support of the Netanyahu government in Israel has perpetuated what Amnesty International in December 2024 labelled a genocide of Palestinian people in Gaza. No amount of finger-pointing at Green candidate Jill Stein or the voters of Michigan can obscure the fact that Democrats refused to listen to their voter base or to uphold even the remnants of the "rules-based international order" that Biden promised to restore. The consequences of that failure – for American democracy and for the world – are, even now, difficult to fathom.

One was that Trump was given ample room to market himself, again, as the "anti-war" candidate. During the campaign, Trump said repeatedly that neither the October 7 attacks nor the invasion of Ukraine would have happened on his watch. Neither is a defensible position: Trump's approach to the Middle East and Israel arguably emboldened extremism in Israel, while the Abraham Accords, constructed in part by Trump's son-in-law Jared Kushner, cornered Palestinians. And Trump has already made it clear that, as far as he is concerned, Putin can do whatever he wants. But to Americans exhausted by endless conflicts and imperialism, Trump's lines were, and remain, understandably appealing.

Trump is not an isolationist, and he is not anti-war

The reality is that Trump is not an isolationist, and he is not anti-war. Trump may well withdraw the United States from NATO, as he has repeatedly threatened. But he will continue to enjoy parades on the Champs-Élysées, to engage with European leaders, to make spectacles out of his "deals" with dictators, and to threaten to annex the Panama Canal, Greenland and Canada, and "take over" the Gaza Strip. That is not isolationism. It is just a different exercise of American power, now speaking the language of naked, violent imperialism.

With few exceptions, Trump and the people he has surrounded himself with are not anti-war. They are against specific types of war. They might be more reluctant to risk American lives – though even that is unclear – but they are not ideologically opposed to violent conflict more broadly. Project 2025, the Heritage Foundation's detailed plan for the second Trump administration, recommends increasing American force strength by up to 50,000 troops – troops that, they argue, should be stationed in the Asia-Pacific. Despite Trump's unconvincing denials to the contrary, many of Project 2025's architects have joined the administration, and he is signing the executive orders they have drafted for him. And his hawkish cabinet shares their views, especially on China.

Trump and Vice President J.D. Vance might claim that the conflict in Syria after the fall of Assad is "not our fight", but they have no objection to American-supplied bombs being dropped on Syria or Lebanon by Israeli jets. The second Trump administration will continue to offer full-throated American support to Israel. Within the administration, that support is primarily motivated not by calculation but by ideological evangelism.

Trump does not abhor violence. He loves it, as he plumps his own macho image. A failure to understand that, and the role played by China hawks in Trump's cabinet, may lead to grave miscalculations in China and the region more broadly.

Trump's trade war on China will have global reverberations. While there has been some justifiable scepticism about Trump's bluster, and it is possible that he will seek out some kind of detente with President Xi Jinping, his cabinet choices suggest otherwise. His picks for Secretary of State, Secretary of Defense, CIA Director and other key national security positions all point to conflict escalation. Those figures, and the underlings drawn from the movement behind Project 2025, see the United States as engaged in an existential conflict with China. To them, China represents an unacceptable threat to American primacy. In that mindset, war is understood as inevitable and necessary.

This is the context in which the future of AUKUS must be understood. As the Congressional Research Service has made clear, no US administration is likely to hand over those Virginia-class submarines, due both to practical issues with manufacturing capacity and to political considerations. But the Trump administration is unlikely to abandon the AUKUS pact altogether. There's no reason to think the president would not be amenable to basing US nuclear submarines in Australian ports, or to continuing to take eye-watering amounts of Australian money with no strings attached. The risks of subordinating Australian sovereignty and agency to a Trump administration, or to whatever comes next, are considerable.

It should go without saying that primacy at any cost is not a strategy. Nor is blind adherence to US primacy by its allies. Supporting it unconditionally puts Australia in the perverse position of having to maintain an alliance with a great protector that deliberately escalates the chances of a catastrophic conflict – into which our government could cravenly consign us, and in which there would be no protection and no winners.

Daddy is not coming to save us. He is putting us in danger.

Finding our voice

We do not, in fact, need saving at all – especially not by that man, to channel former prime minister Julia Gillard. But that does not leave us alone, without options. Quite the opposite.

Trump might not abandon the AUKUS pact, but he will abandon the Pacific. The few specifics we have about his administration's foreign policy suggest that it will treat the Pacific as nothing more than a staging ground for its "great-power competition" games with China – much as previous administrations, and Australian governments, have done, though perhaps with less pretence.

Trump does not care if Pacific island states are drowned by rising sea levels. His administration will do everything possible to ensure that those sea levels rise faster than they already are. It has already withdrawn (already inadequate) American aid, and will certainly not honour the Biden administration's promise to continue to recognise Pacific statehood even in the event that Pacific territory disappears. His mass deportations will also impact thousands of Filipinos and Pacific islanders.

These rapidly changing and volatile regional circumstances raise significant questions for Australia. If the United States under Trump further turns its back, to whom might Pacific island leaders turn for support? The Albanese government, just like the Morrison government before it, continues to talk up its Pacific engagement strategy. But an uncritical closeness to the Trump administration risks further pushing the Pacific – "our family", as Minister Pat Conroy, channelling his predecessor, Senator Concetta Fierravanti-Wells, blithely calls them – away.

Contrary to the actions of the China hawks and their talk of "appeasement", engagement and partnership with Pacific island nations requires much more than the occasional bilateral security agreement or grant for a football team. It means a genuine commitment to collective security – not simply talking about support for climate mitigation in the Pacific and then turning around and trumpeting increased gas exports and approving a new coalmine at home. It means significant additional investment in the health, education and wellbeing of the peoples of the Pacific. It means recognising that human security is the wellspring of national security. It means, above all, an Australia acting in its own interests and in the interests of the region – not one that assumes that our interests and those of Trump's America are inextricably aligned. Because they are not.

Trump does not care about us, so why should we care about him?

None of that implies that the interests of many Americans who do not live in that version of the United States, Pacific islanders and

Australians are *not* aligned. In courting Trump, the Australian government risks undermining the shared interests that transcend specific administrations in democracy and collective security. There is a solidarity to be found between actual people over their governments – a solidarity that might build genuine security and help stave off the worst excesses of an increasingly totalitarian White House.

Writing in *Foreign Affairs* in December 2024, Nancy Okail and Matthew Duss of the Center for International Policy, a Washington DC think tank, offered a blueprint for building that kind of solidarity domestically and internationally. This would require a radically different approach to international affairs, one that focuses on cooperation on climate change and other universal public goods like healthcare, development assistance, international law and a commitment to transparency and accountability. This approach recognises that there are no clean dividing lines between domestic policy and foreign policy, or between the values that underpin them – each reflects the other. As Duss and Okail argue:

> Americans must choose between integrity or corruption, accountability or complicity, impunity or the rule of law. These choices are stark, and making the right ones will require real political courage, leadership, and coalition-building. But ultimately, this is the only way to ensure the future of a United States and a world that are safer, more prosperous, and freer.

Australians, too, have some stark choices ahead. Making the same kinds of choices we made during the first Trump administration will not make us, or the world, safer.

It is entirely possible to make different choices. And we would not be alone if we did.

In November 2024, when Trump threatened Canada and Mexico with those blanket tariffs, Justin Trudeau raced to Florida to kiss the ring, just as the Australian prime minister would likely have done. But Trudeau's counterpart in Mexico made a different choice. Instead of scrambling, President Claudia Sheinbaum responded with unapologetic firmness. A trade war, she made clear, was in no one's interests. Sheinbaum refused the temptation to bend to Trump's will, clearly and succinctly outlining American complicity in crises of mobility, drugs and human rights. "What is needed," Sheinbaum argued, "is cooperation and mutual understanding to tackle these significant challenges."

Sheinbaum and Trump later spoke on the phone. In the process, Sheinbaum demonstrated that it is possible to engage with Trump's America without succumbing to fear or appeasement, and without compromising on national interests or values, or on solidarity with the most vulnerable in both places.

It is about time that Australia recognises that it has national power, and lots of it. But such power is useless if our government is incapable of using the agency it gives them to act decisively in our own interest, while contributing to the regional and global security that everyone so desperately seeks.

Trump does not care about us, so why should we care about him? Cosying up to him does not make Australia safer.

We are not powerless. Australia can exercise its agency by connecting directly and building partnerships with those who have an interest in democracy and democratic institutions, among elected representatives at all levels, in the courts, and in civil society – here and in the United States. We can use our diplomatic strength to shore up and uphold the institutions and practices of international law. We can focus on the things that really do make us safer. We can continue to ask ourselves: what might we do in the world if we weren't so afraid? ■

NO DEAL

Why Trump is bad for the economy

Susan Stone

With the return of Donald Trump to the White House, there is a sense that things will go "back to what they should be". Many of his opponents have greeted his presidency with resignation – a belief that the United States weathered his first term and will do so again. His supporters believe not only that the "success" he had in his first administration will be recreated, but that this time his achievements, with both houses of Congress behind him, will be exponentially greater. And while reduced taxes, lower regulation and increased drilling may lead to short-term economic gains, increased deficits, less accountability and higher wage costs will undermine long-term economic growth and prosperity.

The truth of the matter is that the economic outcomes of his first administration were limited: many households were actually worse off at the end of his first term. Trump's mishandling of the COVID-19 pandemic set the US economy back, and the so-called trade deal with China signed in January 2020, which Trump called "a momentous step – one that has never been taken before with China – toward a future of fair and reciprocal trade", was never actually implemented. It is therefore reasonable to question whether the coming changes in the second administration will provide benefits to the US consumer or to the broader global trading system. Despite all his bluster and bravado, Trump 1.0 took the economy backwards – and he is on track to do it again.

China and the protectionist backlash

Long before Trump became a presidential candidate, there was a growing general disillusionment with "globalisation", and an associated perception of a loss of control over economic outcomes as the spread of production across the globe meant less control by any one nation. COVID-19 simply accelerated these trends. When China became a member of the World Trade Organization (WTO) in 2001 and fully entered the global trading system, many economists, me included, felt great hope for the future. It was argued that rising living standards and exposure to overseas ideas would lead naturally to a more liberalised China, with literally billions of consumers ready to buy foreign goods and services. Indeed, China's standard of living increased dramatically during this period: it rose from the sixth-largest to the second-largest economy in the world and eradicated extreme poverty – defined as individuals living on less than US$2 day – within its borders.

But not everything has gone to plan. China's dominance of global value chains and exports helped drive manufacturing jobs out of Western countries. China's subsidies for key industries helped its companies gain footholds and then dominate markets and drive out global competitors. And while these trends have led to lower prices for consumers across the globe, they have also led to whole industries disappearing in many Western economies. A study by Massachusetts Institute of Technology economist David Autor estimates that between 1999 and 2011, trade with China cost the United States 2.4 million jobs, with almost a million of those coming from the manufacturing sector. Autor argues that manufacturing jobs are geographically concentrated and hard to replace. And while trade with China stimulated the creation of other US jobs, these were located in different parts of the country and benefited highly educated, tech-savvy workers. This created a divide between those who were benefiting from growing trade with China and those who were suffering.

The impact of China's rise has been felt beyond the United States. Manufacturing sectors such as whitegoods, automobiles, steel and shipbuilding have been undermined in many industrial countries through Chinese competition, supported by Chinese subsidies. A recent IMF working paper found that roughly 95 per cent of all trade-distorting subsidies imposed between 2009 and 2022 were implemented by China.

The impact of these subsidies depends both on the sector and on the trade partners. The IMF reports that Chinese exports in sectors benefiting from subsidies have a larger impact on G20 Emerging Economies. On the import side, G20 Advanced Economies – which includes Australia – experience a decrease in their exports to China in subsidised sectors of between 3 and 5 per cent.

The perceived success of this strategy for China and the apparent inability of the WTO to address nations' concerns have led to a rise in what could be characterised as tit-for-tat protectionism and subsidies regimes. According to the *Global Trade Alert*, the rate at which protectionist measures have been implemented has increased twelve-fold in recent years, rising from 353 in 2009 to almost 4200 in 2023. Subsidies make up almost half of these measures, while export-related subsidies account for almost 15 per cent and tariffs close to 9 per cent.

This wave of protectionism was kicked off by Trump's initial trade war with China. This began with the 2018 imposition of trade remedies (actions against imports, usually tariffs, which are deemed to be harming a domestic industry) on imports of washing machines and solar panels. China then imposed tariffs on US sorghum, while South Korea launched a WTO dispute on these tariffs. The United States then imposed tariffs on steel and aluminium on national security grounds. While most countries were able to negotiate some exemptions, Australia was the only major US trade partner in these goods for which tariffs were not imposed.

The United States continues to use tariffs, or the threat of them, as well as export controls, to protect key sectors. The Biden administration began to use subsidies as well. And in this regard, the Americans are in good company. The rise of the concept of "friendshoring" – trying to bring back manufacturing in key sectors either to domestic shores or to "friendly" trading partners – was endorsed in 2022 by then Treasury secretary Janet Yellen, who discussed the need to take a "dual" approach in tackling supply-chain disruption and strengthening economic resilience. This led to both the *CHIPS and Science Act* and the *Inflation Reduction Act*, which contain heavy incentives for American companies to cooperate with nations that have US trade agreements to secure semiconductor supply chains and telecommunications networks and the production of renewable energy technologies. Similarly, Japan created a fund for the relocation of production facilities from China back home or to "friendlier" South-East Asian nations. The European Union has approved a series of projects under its "Important Projects of Common European Interest" program to ensure greater supply-chain resilience. Australia is expecting to spend $23 billion on incentives to promote the domestic renewable energy sector in its "Future Made in Australia" policy. Finally, back in 2015, China put forward the "dual circulation strategy", which embedded the idea of China becoming a self-sufficient nation. The strategy was accompanied by the launch of China's industrial policy masterplan, "Made in China 2025".

Research has shown that these policies tend to be expensive and counterproductive. The *Global Trade Alert* found that they tend to play off each other. For example, the European Union has implemented a subsidy response within two years of either China or the United States undertaking similar policies. Trying to out-subsidise sectors simply leads to less efficient outcomes, distorting investment and trade.

Tariffs under Trump 1.0

With hindsight, the consensus is that the Trump tariffs and the subsequent trade deal with China were a net loss to the US economy. And while the tariffs did have an impact on China's economy, it was able to source most of its US imports from other economies, including Australia. However, they also led to widespread retaliation. China, India, Turkey, the European Union and Canada, unable to fully negotiate exemptions from the United States, imposed tariffs of their own.

The third-party effects were also significant. In the first six months of the steel tariffs, smaller developing countries experienced a 12 per cent decline in steel exports to the United States and a 16 per cent decline in revenue. When the Chinese retaliated against American farmers, it increased competition for Australian agricultural goods in other markets, such as the European Union, as US producers sought to replace the Chinese market. While the United States' "Phase 1" deal with the Chinese included commitments to purchase an additional US$200 billion of goods, mostly agricultural, this never did occur.

By any measure, the trade policies implemented by the first Trump administration were not a success. The trade deficit with China was virtually unchanged between 2016 and the end of 2019, and was higher over this period than it was during the preceding Obama administration. And while the bilateral deficit with China was reduced in 2019, the overall US deficit did not fall, as imports were simply diverted to other trade partners.

The impact on the US domestic economy was significant. Estimates are that almost 300,000 jobs were lost, and that the United States lost an estimated 0.3 per cent of GDP. In addition, studies have shown that it was primarily US companies that paid for the US tariffs, with estimated costs of nearly US$46 billion. A further study found that US companies lost at least US$1.7 trillion in their stock value by the end of 2020 as a result of the tariffs.

It is difficult to quantify the impact on Australia of this first round of trade disputes between China and the United States. As noted above, Australia was not targeted in the more sector-specific approach undertaken by the Trump administration. And while some Australian exports may have been displaced by US exports, Chinese economic growth was not significantly impacted and Australian exports to China increased 26 per cent between 2017–18 and 2018–19. Impacts after this cannot be disentangled from those of the COVID-19 pandemic and the subsequent trade tensions between China and Australia.

Trump 2.0

The second Trump administration has doubled down on this approach of using tariffs to drive its trade agenda. Instead of targeting sectors, Trump is proposing across-the-board tariff increases on all imports, with higher rates on Chinese imports. It is fully expected that individual countries will need to negotiate their own way out of these tariffs, and that those with a trade surplus are the primary target. That, in addition to China, includes India, South Korea, Japan, Mexico,

Canada, Taiwan, Vietnam, Germany and Ireland. Indeed, Trump has already announced 25 per cent tariffs on Mexico and Canada and 10 per cent on China. Many of these countries are major trading partners of Australia. If the tariffs significantly affect growth in these countries, this will reduce the amount of goods and services they buy from Australia. Some affected countries are also competitors of Australia (for example, Canada in the wheat sector). If these countries lose access to the US market, they will then compete with Australia in third-country markets, potentially hurting our producers.

The direct impact of any tariffs on Australia is likely to be limited. First, the US accounts for only about 5 per cent of the Australian export market. In addition, the value added of US imports in Australian final demand – that is, the amount of imported goods and services that go into the production of goods sold in Australia – is only around 1 per cent, compared with over 6 per cent added value of Chinese imports.

Some sectors may be more directly affected, however. Beef exports to the United States have been increasing in the past three years, growing from 17 per cent of total exports in 2020 to 23 per cent in 2023. More importantly, the tariffs could hinder Australia's ambitions to diversify its export base and gain a foothold in higher-value-added sectors. While the United States doesn't import much of Australia's traditional commodity market, it does import a lot – as much as 60 per cent – of higher technology goods.

For instance, the United States accounts for 40 per cent of high-tech engine exports, 50 per cent in aircraft and space parts, and almost

60 per cent in machine tools. In addition, the United States is Australia's second-largest services export market, accounting for more than 10 per cent of the total services trade. Professional and technical services, and other business services (such as operational leasing) were Australia's top two exports to the United States in 2023, surpassing beef and gold sales.

But it is not just services exports that matter. We know that, on average, the share of value of services in goods exports is close to 50 per cent. Thus, services play a key role in goods trade, especially in higher-value-added and technology goods.

As it did during Trump's first administration, raising tariffs will cause other countries to retaliate. We have already seen Mexico and Canada announce retaliatory tariffs. In addition, the rising tide of protectionism lends further credibility to other countries following a similar approach. The global impact of the tariffs – such as rising shipping costs, increased US dollar volatility and a general increase in risk from the uncertainty generated from Trump's policies – will flow on to Australia. Trade is a major part of the Australian economy, accounting for as much as 45 per cent of GDP. When the costs associated with doing business internationally grow, it impacts Australian businesses and consumers. When Trump raised tariffs on China in 2018, ocean container shipping market rates spiked more than 70 per cent. Any such increase now would be on top of the recent shipping rate rises due to the conflicts in Europe and the Middle East. For a country as far away from major markets as Australia, higher shipping costs puts our goods at a significant price disadvantage.

Recent OECD estimates project that Australia could lose close to 1.2 per cent of GDP if there were a 10 per cent reduction in trade among major economies. This would mainly be through declines in the mining sector's exports to China. And while a 10 per cent across-the-board US tariff would impact trade, it is unlikely to result in a 10 per cent reduction in global trade. The World Bank estimated that the first trade war led to a 2 per cent reduction in global trade.

Large tariffs on our trading partners, especially China, could slow their growth, which in turn could slow imports of critical Australian goods such as iron ore. More broadly, Trump officials have indicated that the degree to which the administration will impose tariffs depends on individual trading partners, which could lead to a race to the bottom as nations compete to secure access to US markets. Finally, any trade deal with China in the face of these tariffs is likely to involve agriculture, which could significantly impact Australian farmers.

Such instability means the world needs a stable institutional structure to enforce the rules of global trade. Yet the Trump administration threatens this as well.

Divided trading world

Growing frustration with the WTO – over its slow pace in furthering trade liberalisation, its perceived judicial overreach and its seeming inability to deal effectively with China's subsidies regime – has led many countries, especially the United States, to move away from the institution. The use of free trade agreements to make headway on key issues of trade, including labour, environment, intellectual property and the digital economy, has grown markedly over the past fifteen years. This is especially true of large plurilateral – or optional – agreements.

Increasing geopolitical rivalry between the United States and China and shifts in the structure of the global economy (the rise of large emerging economies) have led to substantive disagreements between large actors within the institution. This has affected the WTO's consensus-driven approach to dealmaking. Key among these disagreements are issues with the dispute settlement mechanism, mainly revolving around what the United States considers judicial overreach by the body. This dispute will not be resolved without agreement between the major trading powers, which is unlikely to happen under a Trump administration.

A Republican majority in Congress could raise the spectre of a US withdrawal from the WTO. Trump, in his last administration, threatened to pull out of the organisation if it didn't "shape up". That, coupled with the likely retaliatory reaction of most trading partners to Trump's tariffs, could induce deep divides in the global trading system, undoing years of hard-earned agreements for freer trade. With the United States flouting the WTO's rules, it becomes increasingly difficult to enforce those rules on other nations. For a small open economy like Australia, which has little market power in its own right, this could mean less access to an arbitrator who can defend Australia's rights. For instance, in a ruling in 2021, the WTO agreed with Australia (along with Brazil and Guatemala) that India was unlawfully subsiding its sugar producers. It was a major win for Australia's sugar producers.

There is an urgent need for renewed substantive rulemaking within the WTO. Although the use of trade sanctions for political ends is not new, the United States has been a recent outlier in using its trade policy as a stick to induce changes in foreign economic policies and to enforce what it regards as its trade rights. Now the European Union, which recently released a proposal to achieve strategic economic autonomy, is beginning to move in this direction as well.

Domestic fallout

Trump's tariffs will have significant domestic impacts. Other than the direct impact on consumer prices, imports account for an important share of the value of exports. For instance, German components imported to South Carolina manufacturing plants are put into vehicles that are then exported. Imports account for around 8 per cent of all US exports. However, it is much higher for specific goods. For example, 30 per cent of petroleum and coal exports are made up of imported goods, such as Canadian crude oil; imported goods account for 33 per cent of the value of light trucking and utility vehicle exports. Thus, US producers will suffer both from increasing input costs and from a decline in export competitiveness.

Trump has long argued that tariffs not only deliver revenue but increase foreign investment as businesses try to "tariff-jump". This strategy has been used by the United States in the past – think 1980s Japanese automotive manufacturing investment. More recently, the Biden administration raised import barriers in an effort to boost foreign investment in products such as solar wafers, polysilicon and tungsten.

However, the extent to which tariffs lead to more investment is an open question. Looking at the tariff increases from Trump's first term, greenfield foreign investment initially increased but then fell. In addition, of the US$36 billion of foreign investment announced in 2018, only US$30 billion was committed. The majority of targeted sectors actually experienced a slower rate of investment growth. The fact is that foreign investment is more influenced by factors such as policy stability, infrastructure and skills availability – issues that have increasingly plagued the US manufacturing sector. Addressing these shortfalls has not been discussed as part of Trump's economic plan for 2025 and beyond.

The Trump campaign has promised major tax reductions across the board, including a reduction in the corporate tax rate to 15 per cent. It has been estimated that this, and other policies, will increase the US debt by US$7.8 trillion. And if the US government is borrowing a lot more money in the future, this will drive up prices for other borrowers, including the Australian government. This is of key concern, given Australia's deteriorating budget position.

Trump's tax plan is also likely to put pressure on the domestic economy, as lowering taxes generally stimulates demand. The proposed rollback of regulation will lead to increasing competition for funds as businesses expand their activities. Together, this spells an increase in spending from the private sector, on top of the spending projected for the public sector. But the additional demand may also face a stagnant supply, given the likely reduction in imports and cost increases projected as a result of tariffs, as any business expansion will take time to come online. Thus, while the US inflationary picture has improved markedly, it is not on a solid footing. Pressure on prices is likely as demand outstrips supply. Even if domestic firms can fill the gap of reduced imports, history has shown that they're likely to increase their prices as a result of these policies.

Another factor likely to affect the competitiveness and cost structure of US firms is Trump's immigration policy. Trump has pledged to engage in mass deportation of the estimated 11 million illegal immigrants currently in the United States. This policy will not only be expensive, pumping more money into the economy, but will undermine access to the labour on which many industries depend. Undocumented workers are estimated to make up 42 per cent of US farmworkers. Other sectors with a significant estimated number of undocumented workers include construction (13 per cent), hospitality (7 per cent) and cleaners (24 per cent). No doubt these sectors will demand some government action to counter these impacts, which could lead to further protectionism, additional spending and more inflationary pressure.

Rising inflation in the United States ultimately leads to rising costs around the globe, including in Australia. US buyers push up prices, shipping firms raise fees and companies face greater competition in capital markets. The inevitability of US rate rises in the face of inflation will trigger money flowing into the country, raising the value of the US dollar and the costs in other countries, as many firms borrow and trade in the currency. Australia will be no exception.

Potentially frustrating these trends is Trump's threat regarding the US dollar's role as a reserve currency. While the dollar's role in commodity pricing, including agriculture, has recently come into question, it still has a strong role in the trade of these goods. Deliberate manipulation of the dollar could, at the very least, spell instability in these markets and greater fiscal uncertainty for Australia.

Australia can gain from Trump's folly

The Trump administration's economic agenda – lowering taxes, raising tariffs, subverting key international agreements and moving away from a global approach to trade rules in favour of one-on-one negotiations – will impact global and Australian markets in three significant ways. A large increase in US public debt and investment could trigger renewed inflation and impact global interest rates; an increase in US tariffs, especially against China, could create major disruptions in global value chains and result in slower global growth; and a further withdrawal of US leadership in global affairs could lead to an undermining of the rules-based system and a further weakening of the WTO.

We can expect these events to unfold rapidly. During Trump's first year in office, he renegotiated the North American Free Trade Agreement (as it was then known), implemented a sweeping tax overhaul (which expires in 2025, but which he then plans to make permanent), gave the Department of Homeland Security more latitude to make deportations and arrests of unauthorised migrants, and implemented the first round of tariffs on solar panels and washing machines. In 2025, he has had four additional years to prepare and Republicans now control both houses of Congress, so it is likely that a similarly aggressive policy schedule will be attempted. Indeed, Trump signed forty-five executive orders in his first week in office. While he didn't establish tariffs in his first days in office, he started the machinery to put them in place, beginning with his America First Trade Policy Memorandum. This memo addresses "unfair and unbalanced trade" and establishes an "External Revenue Service" to collect tariffs and other charges, a function currently handled by US Customs and Border Protection, a Department of Homeland Security agency.

Trump assumes that imports will remain relatively unchanged in the face of tariffs, providing revenue. However, a basic tenet of economics is that when the price goes up, demand goes down. Thus, it is much more likely that imports into the United States will fall. And that the United States will face significant retaliatory measures.

But the bigger misconception is that the underlying "problem" that Trump is trying to address with US trade partners, especially China – that of large trade surpluses – will be reversed. Trade deficits are driven more by incomes than by exports. Even if Trump were able to reduce the deficit with China, it would simply move that deficit to other countries, which is exactly what happened last time. Trade deficits reflect a domestically driven gap between spending and production and are largely transmitted through the capital account.

Thus, they are structural domestic imbalances: looking at any one bilateral relationship is like expecting to have a level table after shortening one leg.

If the United States is using more goods through consumption and investment than it produces, it needs to import the rest. If China is using less than it is producing, it exports. Thus, China exports its excess savings to the United States to cover the Americans' shortfall. Unless the United States starts saving more than it is spending, it doesn't matter whether the deficit is covered by China or another country – it still needs to be covered. Tariffs aren't going to change this basic relationship. Even if it manifests as higher domestic investment, it's still spending that needs to come from somewhere. And while tariffs will certainly increase the cost of, and thus reduce, imports, they are also likely to lead to a reduction in exports, especially given the large share of trade in intermediate goods in the US economy. And that is what happened to the United States between 2018 and 2020 (acknowledging that the big dip in trade in 2020 was affected by the global pandemic): both imports and exports fell.

While reductions in tax and regulation lead to lower costs for business, tariffs and potential labour shortages mean higher costs. Which of these dominates depends on myriad factors and the reaction of trading partners. No matter what the specific outcomes of the economic policies of Trump's second term, there will be a rise in market uncertainty and risk. That is always expensive for business. It also may mean that more businesses choose not to trade with US companies, given the policy and regulatory uncertainty surrounding not just the incoming administration but what may follow it. If the pendulum swings away from the populist economic policies currently in vogue, that will mean an unwinding of much of the deregulation and tax breaks expected to be implemented in the next few years. It remains an open question as to whether firms will invest millions or even billions of dollars in facilities in the United States if the costing assumptions on which they are based might not be valid in another four years.

But the outlook might not be all doom and gloom for Australia. First, Australia is a "trusted" partner and has strong defence ties with the United States. Political tensions over Taiwan and the South China Sea are factors that will act in Australia's negotiating favour. In addition, China may prove to be an even bigger market for Australian agricultural goods if, as almost certainly will happen, China retaliates in this sector against the United States. And these market opportunities may go beyond China, as countries find themselves on the wrong end of US trade policy. Australia might gain in the areas of tourism and education as a less volatile alternative. Finally, in the growing global competition for skilled talent, Australia can put its people forward as a strong US substitute, as well as being a more attractive location for third-country talent.

Trump's economic policies are based on flawed assumptions and could do significant damage to the US and global economies. But this could also be a golden moment for Australian business. ■

THE AMBASSADORS' BRIEFINGS

Australia's three previous ambassadors to Washington report on how to deal with the Trump administration

Kim Beazley

Ambassador to the United States 2010–2016

The new Trump administration will not replicate the first. Under the first administration, appointments, policies and budgets were largely linked to what had gone before. The experience infuriated Trump supporters. Many of his new appointments share his disruptive instincts. The extent to which they share his punitive vengefulness is not yet knowable.

Trump is also now much more knowledgeable about utilising the levers of power. His preoccupation is domestic. In his view, that is where his enemies are. His message for America's adversaries is that he is not looking for a military fight. But he is good for an economic fight with everyone on tariffs, and with allies on fiscal burden sharing, particularly defence budgets.

Australia successfully negotiated away Trump's proposed steel and aluminium tariffs during his previous administration. But Trump is now more radical in his approach to government. He has nothing to lose and even less affection for US allies and trading partners.

Trump also knows how troubled America's fiscal position is. US public debt is now 123 per cent of GDP. From 1984, the debt grew from US$5 trillion to US$35 trillion. Servicing the debt is becoming the largest single item in the budget. By 2050, if left unchecked, it will be 195 per cent of GDP. Trump has been clear: he values tariffs as much for the revenue they create as for protection of American production. He knows, too, that his determination to re-legislate the sunsetted tax cuts from his last term will be crippling for the deficit and will render his additional promised tax cuts a fiscal nightmare. All this makes it unlikely that his administration will offer tariff relief, even though allies such as Australia have free trade agreements with the United States.

President Biden's administration had a realistic view of the relative decline in American military power. He sought allies to balance China's expanding military power and economic reach. Notably, he was forthright about his willingness to defend Taiwan. Trump leads a party that, in Congress, is fiercely anti-Chinese and will not accept that the United States is not unilaterally powerful militarily. They would commit to Taiwan. Trump would not, and never has in public. This will be a major point of difference between Trump and his legislators.

Another will be the technological component of the competition with China. The ban on sales of US chips to China initiated by the Biden administration has drawn a Chinese ban on sales of germanium, gallium and antimony to America. These minerals are critical in a range of weapons systems. The world has been surprised by Trump's reassertion of a US need to acquire Greenland but it is not simply a strategic geographical concern. Greenland has large quantities of critical minerals, including rare earths, which are essential ingredients in new technology manufacturing.

Trump understands the threat underlying China's massive dominance of global supply and the problems for American industry associated with retaliatory Chinese bans. This is an area where Australia may be invaluable to the Trump administration. Trump might not understand that Australia's geology can supply the West's needs, and that we have the skills to mine and process them. The Australian government has recognised this, moving to provide generous loans to establish a major heavy rare earth processing plant at Eneabba, north of Perth. A conversation with Australia is better than agonising over purchasing or seizing Greenland.

It is highly unlikely that defence spending will survive at current levels, despite Trump's promises

But the Trump administration is showing burgeoning indifference to the United States' relationships with its allies, including their democratic processes. Trump openly rejoiced in and claimed credit for the destruction of the Trudeau government in Canada. And he did not rebuke the extraordinary attacks by Elon Musk on the Starmer government in the United Kingdom.

All this foreshadows a major challenge for Australia's current ambassador, Kevin Rudd, as he attempts to keep our relationship with the United States on an even keel. Prime ministers, presidents and national security ministers, along with their departments, provide the overall direction of the relationship. However, the embassy provides the nuance and detail on what needs to be done, according to the policy directions determined by ministers.

For example, Australia's planned acquisition of US Virginia-class nuclear-powered submarines depends on attitudes within the Congress as well as the US Navy and, broadly, the Pentagon. The vital role of the embassy was evident in the passage of the *National Defense Authorization Act* in December 2023. This enables the sale of the Virginia-class subs to Australia and authorises the training of Australians in submarine maintenance, mandates technology sharing and includes the United Kingdom and Australia in the *Defense Production Act*.

Representative Joe Courtney, who is co-chair of the Friends of Australia Caucus and the AUKUS Working Group, and the ranking member of the Seapower and Projection Forces subcommittee of the Defense Committee of the House, said "getting those provisions through the Congress did not happen by itself. There is no question the intensive effort to educate members of Congress by the embassies of the UK and Australia was instrumental in getting these provisions passed and into law".

More recently, the Australian embassy had to work to point out that the appropriation the administration sought on submarines would have slowed production to a rate that would not have allowed any to be passed on to Australia to meet the 2032–33 deadline. Lobbying went into effect and the funding was increased. Devils in the detail will continue to emerge. These submarines are a vital acquisition for Australia, and it will largely be the task of the embassy to keep the procurement agreement on track.

The so-called Department of Government Efficiency, managed by Elon Musk, will make substantial changes to US spending. It is highly unlikely that defence spending will survive at current levels, despite Trump's promises that it will be increased. As it declines, the argument will be that waste is being cut but meaningful capability is not. This will be a nonsense. The ramifications of loss of capability – particularly to the submarine arm – will need to be closely watched. The Australian embassy is large enough and has sufficient expertise to keep the Australian government well informed.

The embassy will also need to develop a narrative that will be influential with Trump's new team. The issues that emerged in handling Trump 1.0 had to be dealt with by the then prime minister, Malcolm Turnbull, more than by the embassy. Turnbull's methods are worthy of study, but he was helped by long experience in hard negotiations. One negotiation was to persuade Trump – over the objections of his advisers – that he must persist with a previously concluded agreement on the transfer of refugees from Australia to the United States. Another effort, as noted earlier, was for tariff relief.

During those arguments, the embassy kept a focus on Australia's value to the United States. In truth, Australia is the least troublesome high-value ally the United States has. Through the post–World War II era, America's main allies in Europe, the Middle East and the Pacific have imposed a tacit existential penalty on the United States. It remains possible that providing support for those allies risks nuclear devastation or damage on the US mainland. Commitments to Australia do not impose such risks.

On the other hand, Australia has joint US facilities that could be targeted. Unlike when the first of these facilities was constructed, they are now of near irreplaceable value to us, as well as to the United States. Likewise, US systems are more extensively integrated into our strategic and battlefield intelligence, surveillance and targeting. It is a mutually beneficial transaction. We hosted Pine Gap – the largest technological intelligence facility of the United States – and, courtesy of our "full knowledge and consent" principle, Australians are integrated throughout. This point can't be overstated, and the embassy makes this argument in its conversations with the administration and Congress.

The United States also benefits strategically from our geography. As it has come to see China as its pre-eminent competitor, the United States has recognised Australia's value as a location with regional deployment advantages. Access to military facilities in Australia's north and west is emerging as a critical element of the relationship. It is possible to imagine a scenario where American bases in North Asia have gone, and the ability to deploy from Australia is of paramount importance. Without it, the United States would be eliminated from the western Pacific.

The economic relationship is wholly beneficial to the Americans. The trade balance is nearly three to one in favour of the United States. The US invests about US$1.3 trillion in Australia. Australians invest similar totals in the United States. Trump likes arms sales. We buy heavily from US sources, particularly through the RAAF. With AUKUS, we are buying US submarines and providing US$3 billion in investment. The Americans will not be out of pocket.

Australia is the least troublesome high-value ally the United States has

So the Australia–United States relationship is unlikely to be disrupted during Trump's second term. However, Trump's handling of ties in the region and globally could cause collateral damage. AUKUS is not objected to by most Republican legislators or by most in Trump's circle, but it could face challenges because Trump and (in particular) first buddy Elon Musk have taken a dislike to the British government. All allies, including Australia, will be asked to substantially increase their defence expenditures. Responses may not satisfy the administration.

The Australian media will constantly question whether or not Kevin Rudd can function due to his past critical comments about Trump. In this regard he is in company with a large number of Republicans, from Vice President J.D. Vance down. Indeed, Trump appeared to have no knowledge of Rudd's views until alerted by Reform UK party leader Nigel Farage. One suspects that, given what is on Trump's plate, the matter is not likely to be in his focus.

Australia's embassy on Massachusetts Avenue, Washington DC, is experienced and effective. In his second term, Trump will be more disruptive and less predictable, but Australia is well placed to protect and advance its own interests.

Joe Hockey
Ambassador to the United States 2016–2020

American history has lionised the brave disruptors. Think of the Rockefellers, the Gettys, Thomas Edison, the Wright brothers, J.P. Morgan. Across all walks of life for more than 200 years, America has either led dramatic change or been a huge influencer. The emergence of technology companies such as Apple, Microsoft, Google and Tesla over the last four decades proves that the disruption gene continues to thrive.

American politics is no different. Surely, leading a revolutionary army makes George Washington the most significant disruptive force in American politics. Abraham Lincoln led a revolution too. Slavery was widely accepted in the United States in the middle of the 19th century. Lincoln broke the mould by standing up to the economically powerful South. As a result, America went to war with itself, losing more soldiers in the Civil War than in all its other wars combined.

Decades later, another Republican president, Teddy Roosevelt, blew up tradition and community standards. He railed against big business. He gazetted vast tracts of US land to create national parks. Almost everything he advocated for, from racial equality to equal pay for women, was radical in its day.

Others, such as his Democrat cousin Franklin D. Roosevelt, John F. Kennedy and Lyndon Johnson, were disruptors. And, of course, the president who coined the slogan "Make America Great Again", Ronald Reagan, was anything but a conservative. It took great courage to stare down the Soviet Union and bring about the end of the Cold War.

Donald Trump has advocated for radical change to the way Washington DC operates. But his predilection for radical change is far from uncommon in the American political context. His vision is for a very different America to the one he inherited from presidents Joe Biden, Barack Obama, George W. Bush and Bill Clinton. The America that Trump took over on 20 January 2025 was worldly and collegial. That's not Donald Trump. He takes pride in the proclamation "America First".

The United States has for eight decades been a shining beacon, promoting and protecting multilateralism, free trade, democracy and the rule of law. Freedom of speech and of the press are enshrined in America's Constitution, but until the end of World War II the United States was a reluctant global leader. It's blood and gold leadership in the darkest hours of the 1940s thrust the nation into an uncomfortable new role. If not for Harry Truman and Dwight Eisenhower, America might have retreated into splendid isolation once again.

Today, the majority of nations around the world are most comfortable when America is the stable and predictable big brother. Nations have come to expect, and take for granted, that the first point of contact for the settlement of international disputes, from the Middle East to Ukraine and from Haiti to the South China Sea, is Washington DC.

America is expected to throw money and technology at problems ranging from pandemics to refugee displacement, wherever and whenever they occur. But Americans are tired of being expected to solve everyone else's problems. They have paid a heavy price over the last eighty years for being the rest of the world's big brother.

What prior presidents viewed as American leadership Trump views as America in decline. He believes the globalist status quo favours elites in other countries and hands America's wealth to foreigners rather than caring for its own. He recognised that, like in the 1920s and the 1930s, there is a strong desire across America to fix challenges at home before addressing those abroad.

Working-class Americans are tired of being the victims of change. They want to hope that things will get better. They feel that America used to be great for them and their families, but in today's world their ambitions are less achievable and daily life is harder. Moreover, they have a deep distrust of politicians. Words are cheap and cynicism is bountiful.

Americans are tired of being expected to solve everyone else's problems

Trump not only proved to Americans that he hears their concerns, but he has consistently advocated for the solutions that they want to hear. To stop illegal immigrants, he says he will build a wall. To stop unlawful drugs, he says he will be tougher on crime. To lower energy prices, he says, "Drill, baby, drill!" To create more jobs, he says he will make imports more expensive and build factories in America. To lower taxes, he says he will generate more revenue from tariffs.

There is no deep logic to some of these simple solutions. For example, tariffs inevitably end up as a tax on American consumers. They are also highly inflationary. That flows through to higher interest rates and, given the size of US government debt, the interest bill will keep rising. Taxes will go up.

It is, however, a mistake to assume that Trump's policies are radical. Over many years, other presidents have implemented similar programs. Barack Obama deported close to 3 million illegal immigrants over his eight-year presidency. George W. Bush deported perhaps 2 million. Even Joe Biden deported at least half a million during his term in office. So how is Trump's plan radical and harsh?

In international affairs, many presidents have withheld funding from multilateral organisations because their policies were at odds with that of the agencies. Under Obama, the IMF found it near impossible to get support for a new funding round to assist problem economies. And every president in recent times has railed against the underfunding of defence by NATO allies. Donald Trump 1.0 was the only president to get some traction from America's European allies.

Reagan thought a lower tax regime would deliver better budget outcomes – "trickle-down economics". Even George W. Bush imposed tariffs on Australia during a particularly testy moment in the economic relationship.

The difference this time around is that Trump believes America's strength is best served by focusing on domestic issues rather than by creating and protecting a wider marketplace. He does not see the

United States as being the greatest beneficiary of a global order that supports freedom, democracy and the rule of law. Trump is not wedded to a system or tradition. He is therefore willing to take more of a gamble on policy and politics to get the outcome he wants.

All the while, Trump uses more colourful language than anyone. He is a master communicator in a world that uses words and visuals more loosely and aggressively than ever before. Social media has weaponised aggressive, fact-less communication in a way no society before ours has experienced. If you marry Trump's unique communication skills with his pugilistic instincts, then you can see why he has such enormous global cut-through.

While this style can be off-putting for other world leaders (and diplomats), it presents opportunities for new partnerships. Those willing to map out a trade or transaction that serves America's interests and meets Trump's explicit political goals will have a real advantage over the next four years. In the meantime, even his harshest critics have tempered their outrage. Expectations for Trump are high but not startling. His plans will be rolled out at a fast and furious pace.

I expect that the change will be rapid for at least the next eighteen months. Trump will be hamstrung by narrow Republican majorities in the House and the Senate. His budget ambitions will be almost unachievable, but his policy disruption on everything from trade to climate change will be substantial. As his congressional colleagues start looking at a likely Democrat majority in the House in just two years, the radicalisation of American politics by Trump 2.0 will be more complicated.

No matter what, the United States has had "disruptors in chief" before. Its institutions and constitution are robust enough to cope with the strain. The open question, however, is whether Donald Trump will be deserving of his desired carve-out on Mount Rushmore or whether he will be consigned to the inglorious history of failed and forgotten American leaders.

Arthur Sinodinos

Ambassador to the United States 2020–2023

The post-war rules-based order is under unprecedented strain, and not just from Xi Jinping and Vladimir Putin. The advent of Donald Trump means that the principal author of that order, the United States, is also in the business of upending it to better suit American interests and values – as interpreted by him.

The foreign policy of our principal ally might now be "America First", but the question for Australia is what influence we can exert so that it is not "America Only". Should we simultaneously become more self-reliant, carving out a more distinctive role in the evolving world order? Australian policymakers will need a shift in mindset. They should be thinking about how to shape the administration's agenda, rather than merely preparing for what the new administration might do.

As we found during the first Trump term, diplomacy in Washington must operate in a style more akin to that of a private business. When I first arrived in Washington in 2020, one long-serving ambassador told me that the best way to get things done was to go straight to the point person in the White House handling the issue. The Australian embassy will also have to deal with the shadow administration, which will include Republican operatives with longstanding ties to the Trump inner circle and family, as well as business figures. Tech bros such as Elon Musk, who will run the so-called Department of Government Efficiency, loom large too.

Trump 2.0 does not have much time for nuanced statecraft or alliances and treaties. At its core, his foreign policy proceeds from three premises. First, hard power is paramount. Second, domestic interests should drive foreign policy priorities. Third, state-on-state relations are inherently transactional, so interests will always trump values.

President Trump prides himself on being unpredictable, so as to put counterparts on edge and leave them guessing at what he will do. Transactional politics on an industrial scale. Deal-making is paramount.

Trump is committed to no more wars on his watch. He believes in talking loudly and carrying a big stick. His admiration for strongmen such as Xi Jinping reflects a focus on the exercise of hard power.

This is already playing out. Trump threatened Hamas with "hell to pay" if the remaining Israeli hostages were not released by Inauguration Day, 20 January. This was gunboat diplomacy on steroids. It was followed by threatening the BRICS grouping with 100 per cent tariffs if they seek to undermine the standing of the US dollar as the global reserve currency.

The recent tariffs imposed on Mexico, Canada and China, which were linked to Trump's concerns about immigration and fentanyl, demonstrated he is serious, and that has set trading partners and allies on edge. To Trump, "tariff" is the most beautiful word in the English language. It is an all-purpose weapon, to be deployed for economic, social and political ends – a free lunch that encourages onshoring and generates revenue for government. The domestic costs and impacts of tariffs are dismissed as trivial.

Some in Trump world sell tariffs as a social tool to restore a lost way of life, in which American manufacturing and high-paying jobs, often for prime-aged males, meant a secure middle-class lifestyle for families. When Trump reversed the ban on the Keystone Pipeline in 2017, he proudly proclaimed that the steel for the pipeline's construction would be made in the United States, just like it used to be. This appeals to those Americans who have been left behind by rapid globalisation and are suffering from status anxiety, particularly in the "flyover states".

Washington insiders are debating whether Trump will prioritise a universal tariff or more selective measures. Australia is well placed to avoid targeted measures. Like most Americans, Trump is well disposed towards Australia and Australians. Importantly, we have consistently run a trade deficit with the United States, and last time we scored a special deal on steel and aluminium restrictions. Australia can lay the groundwork here by reminding the administration of the facts of our trade relationship, the complementarities between our two economies and our broader alliance contribution.

To Trump, "tariff" is the most beautiful word in the English language

China is the principal target of Trump's tariff agenda, but the end state of US policy is not clear: is it mainly about trade and economic concerns, or a grand strategy that encompasses far-reaching political, technological and military goals (other than a vague wish to remain "number one")? In Trump's first term, trade outcomes were the priority. His administration did, however, move to put more restrictions on technology transfer to, and investment in, China.

Will China hawks such as the Secretary of State (Marco Rubio) and the National Security Advisor (Mike Waltz) throw out the Biden approach of derisking sensitive tech sectors in favour of a more thoroughgoing decoupling? Trump's rhetoric is more consistent with the latter. However, regime change in China – the desired end state of some Republicans – seems off the agenda (and would get little support in this region).

China has been preparing retaliation for tariff increases, including banning export of critical minerals in which it dominates the production process. The Chinese are also honing their negotiating strategy. They could offer a grand bargain that encompasses trade and other issues, including security assurances – say, on the South China Sea and Taiwan. But Trump's last agreement with Xi, in January 2020, failed miserably to counter the trade deficit with China.

For domestic reasons, a deal would appeal to Trump. During the 2024 campaign, he threw shade on Taiwan for allegedly taking the semiconductor industry away from the United States and free-riding on American defence spending. He ducked and weaved on whether he would come to Taiwan's defence in the event of a Chinese attack. But there is a strong constituency for Taiwan in the Republican Party, with some even wanting the United States to go as far as formal recognition. These Republicans would make it difficult for Trump to accept such an offer.

However, allies and partners such as Australia might come under pressure to fall into line with further American sanctions and controls on tech and investment trade with China. The first Trump administration pursued the "Clean Network" initiative to freeze Huawei out of Western telecommunications systems. Australia was ahead of the game, having earlier ruled Huawei out of its 5G mobile network rollout.

This time, further restrictions would create tensions for Australia, which under the Albanese government moved to stabilise the China relationship. Australia can begin by explaining to the United States the comprehensive measures we already have in place to deal with foreign interference in our economy, critical infrastructure, intellectual property, technologies and universities. We can claim to have been ahead of the Americans in policies to counter foreign interference. The conversation should be about where we need to plug holes in existing regimes and to jointly counter trade and economic coercion, rather than blanket exclusions. The Chinese will appreciate the distinction and, in any case, do not want to reprise their "wolf warrior" diplomacy.

Allies and partners may also be asked to spend more on defence, including on foreign military sales from the United States. The price tag for AUKUS may be increased beyond the US$3 billion we will inject into the US submarine industrial base. (We are doing the same in the United Kingdom.)

Australian officials should remind their new American counterparts of the full extent of the recent Australian defence build-up, including AUKUS Pillars 1 and 2, the Guided Weapons Enterprise, the ramping-up of infrastructure and personnel in Northern Australia, as well as the key role of facilities such as Pine Gap in America's military operations and intelligence activities around the world. The conversation can then be about what additional activities are required for us to operate better together, rather than budget aggregates.

We can also review how the reforms to the International Traffic in Arms Regulations and export controls are working, and seek further exemptions to create a defence free trade area with the United States (and United Kingdom). Such an arrangement will make it easier to share platforms, information and technologies, in the interests of interchangeability on the battlefield. These matters are best pursued in the annual Australia–United States Ministerial Consultation (known as "AUSMIN") and framed around countering China.

In Trump world, the fate of regional groupings hangs in the balance. A latticework of mini-laterals has proliferated in the region, most notably among Australia, Japan, Korea, the Philippines, India and the United States. This network is a unique advantage the United States has in facing up to China. The message to the Americans should be based on the mutuality principle: they need us as much as we may need them. The arrangements in the Indo-Pacific are essential to the security of the United States.

After the election, there was a view in Japanese circles that the best way to engage the Trump administration in the Indo-Pacific may be through the Quadrilateral Security Dialogue. This view was vindicated immediately after the president's inauguration when the foreign ministers of Australia, India and Japan met in Washington with newly confirmed Secretary Rubio. Trump may feel a particular sense of ownership of this grouping because he revived it during his first administration. He also has a strong and friendly relationship with Prime Minister Narendra Modi of India. The Quad has been a good vehicle to keep the United States engaged with South-East Asia and the Pacific through the delivery of public goods like vaccines, maritime domain awareness and education fellowships, and has eschewed an explicit security focus. This most recent meeting's communique emphasised the role of the Quad in regional maritime, economic and tech security. The Trump administration is clearly shifting the Quad to have a more overt focus on countering China; the forthcoming leader-level meeting of the Quad will indicate how far this may go.

In Trump world, the fate of regional groupings hangs in the balance

The bottom line for Australia today is that longstanding assumptions about what will capture American interest must be revisited. We can be a strong ally but also, through creative diplomacy, preserve and, where useful, expand regional groupings with like-minded concerns.

Increased self-reliance will give Australia options. And self-reliance is a mindset as much as a set of policies. It means accepting that we are living in a more multipolar world. American exceptionalism and the "light on the hill" will now be in the service of America as just another great power, rather than to enforce a Pax Americana or foster the global order that has been so congenial to like-minded democracies.

Self-reliance in defence means more (targeted) spending, particularly in defence tech innovation, asymmetric strategies that counter the size and tech advantages of potential adversaries and attracting private capital to bolster the defence effort. A more agile, tech-intensive military is in our own interest, as well as that of the alliance. For middle powers such as Australia, it requires a whole-of-society defence posture.

Diplomatic statecraft and an effective military go hand in hand. We need to double down on our relationships with like-minded democracies and our work in ASEAN and the Pacific, but also to engage other non-traditional players. That includes the Global South and groupings in which the United States is not necessarily represented, such as the Commonwealth. Multilateral institutions also need attention, as they are another locus for great-power competition including over important global issues such as who will set the standards that will underpin new technologies and industries.

Self-reliance is not code for "appeasing" China or pivoting to put all our eggs in the China basket. We have stood up to China in recent years and weathered the trade and economic coercion that followed. That is in our DNA. We can handle China best by showing we have options on trade and security partnerships. Self-reliance also means putting our own house in order. We must keep building the strong, resilient economy that will give us the wherewithal to create more necessary flexibility. Defence and international security policy is not a free lunch. ■

THE FIX

Solving Australia's foreign affairs challenges

David Heslop and Joel Keep on How Australia Can Lead a New Era of Non-proliferation

"Australia is well positioned to play a central role in efforts to counter chemical and biological threats in the age of generative AI ... The Australia Group's purview should be expanded to include a select range of biological design tools and other AI software that might aid in the construction of chemical and biological weapons."

THE PROBLEM: In recent years, a number of generative artificial intelligence (AI) platforms have been developed that, their designers claim, will revolutionise work, life and the way people relate to one another. For much of the public, the most familiar systems have been the large language models (LLMs) that use machine-learning techniques to generate text, and similar platforms that can create (less convincing) imagery. However, the AI systems of most interest to chemical and biological researchers are the suite of biological design tools, LLM-powered chemistry agents and other platforms that can be applied to the life sciences.

Biological design tools will be crucial to advances that could greatly benefit human health in the coming years. The tools used for understanding complex molecular structures – such as the AlphaFold series, which can predict the shape of proteins based on their amino acid sequence – have already demonstrated great potential for aiding our understanding of human disease. AI-powered chemistry aids, such as Coscientist, are helping design new generations of life-saving drugs, and there are multiple applications for AI in radiology, neuroimaging and the wider biomedical field.

However, this emerging suite of AI platforms might be misused by those seeking a biological or chemical method for causing harm to humans. Since the advent of genetic engineering in the 1970s, concerns have been raised that advances in biotechnology might be used in the weaponisation of pathogens or toxins. These fears returned when advances in synthetic biology in the 2000s accelerated alongside anxieties over bioterrorism, following the anthrax attacks in the United States. The COVID-19 pandemic, the acute phase of which ended just as this new era of generative AI began, is a more recent reminder of the destruction an infectious biological agent can cause, whatever its provenance.

THE PROPOSAL: Australia, which has a long history of helping build the global non-proliferation architecture, is well positioned to play a central role in efforts to counter chemical and biological threats in the age of generative AI. After chemical weapons were unleashed on soldiers and civilians during the Iran–Iraq War in the 1980s, the Department of Foreign Affairs established the Australia Group (AG), which set out to prevent further proliferation of this heinous class of weapons. Initially the group was concerned with harmonising regulations on the export of chemical precursors for nerve agents, vesicants and other chemical weapons that devastated the Iran–Iraq frontline. In short order, the AG, whose forty-three members now include the United States, the European Union, India, Japan and the United Kingdom, expanded its remit to include biological weapons.

The AG's purview should now be expanded to include a select range of biological design tools and other AI software that might aid in the construction of chemical and biological weapons. This need not include all AI systems with scientific utility, most of which will be of great benefit to humanity. Rather, a select few AI platforms – those that are capable of enhancing pathogens with pandemic potential – should be subject to greater scrutiny: specifically, systems that may be able to increase the virulence or transmissibility of an infectious biological agent, or that may allow a pandemic pathogen to evade established medical countermeasures, undermine human immunity or escape detection.

At the time of writing, there is no consensus in the biosecurity community on a standardised approach to the evaluation – or "red teaming" – of biological design tools: in other words, how to safely and effectively establish precisely what they are capable of. Most evaluations have so far been conducted on an ad-hoc basis, pushed along by non-profits such as the Nuclear Threat Initiative's "NTI | bio" group. To address this, the federal government should create an Australian AI safety institute of the type first established in the United Kingdom following the AI Safety Summit held at Bletchley Park in November 2023. Expertise could be leveraged from the CSIRO and the Defence Science and Technology Group, both of which have staff experienced in chemical and biological security. The institute could help formulate methods for red teaming AI platforms that may have dangerous applications.

WHY IT WILL WORK: While the emerging capabilities of biological design tools and AI-powered chemistry aides might sound alarming, there is a great difference between producing something *in silico* – that is, through computational modelling – and turning it into a deployable weapon in the real world. Such threats remain digital until they are turned into physical biological agents that can sicken or infect human beings. For this reason, most biosecurity professionals have emphasised the importance of securing the "digital-to-physical frontier" of synthetic biology and AI.

Here, the AG can play an essential role by building on previous initiatives seen in the United States. In October 2023, the Biden administration unveiled Executive Order 14110, which laid a foundation for establishing the safe and secure use of artificial intelligence. The order tasked the Department of Energy with developing model evaluations and guardrails for emergent AI platforms with biological applications. Crucially, the administration also constructed a new framework for the management of nucleic acid synthesis technology, the machinery used to manipulate DNA and RNA, the genetic building blocks of the life sciences. Historically, DNA synthesisers have been prohibitively expensive, and most are housed in secure laboratory settings. However, advances in this technology are ushering in an era of "benchtop" synthesis, in which such work is conducted on much smaller machines and for a fraction of the cost.

The Biden administration accurately identified the combination of artificial intelligence and benchtop synthesis technology as a tangible pathway to making pathogens that could unleash great harm. Nucleic acid assembler and synthesiser technology is already a target of the AG. There remain, however, gaps in the group's coverage that will likely soon be filled by biological design tools and adjacent AI platforms. Resolving these vulnerabilities will require constant vigilance as advances in artificial intelligence continue.

Biden's executive order, however, was swiftly jettisoned by the second Trump administration upon taking office in January 2025. At the time of writing, the Stargate initiative, which replaced the order, does not feature any equivalent safeguards. This makes the preservation of Biden's initiative a pressing concern for the international community, if we are to avoid the weaponisation of AI in the coming years. The AG could serve as a forum for both preserving and promoting the essence of Biden's initiative.

Before embarking on this diplomatic initiative, however, Australia must get its house in order. A first step would be the adoption of federal legislation based on Biden's executive order. A second line of effort is the creation of an Australian AI safety institute to assess AI platforms. AI designers have conducted their own risk assessments, but these are vulnerable to internal commercial influence. Australia could act as neutral ground for evaluating AI models that have potential biosecurity risks.

There are, of course, no guarantees in preventing the misuse of AI platforms with chemical and biological applications. AI's centre of gravity will remain in the United States, where the industry is fast accruing political leverage that will challenge any new regulatory framework the Trump administration might consider. More ambitious strategies that tap into the convergent promise of chemistry, synthetic biology and AI will need to be embraced. Australia – and all of those invested in the international non-proliferation architecture – will need to find ways of preventing a new generation of chemical and biological weapons from being unleashed, and to keep the balance of risk tipped in favour of global health security. ■

Reviews

CHINA

On Xi Jinping: How Xi's Marxist Nationalism Is Shaping China and the World
Kevin Rudd
Oxford University Press

I admit coming to this book as a sceptic, although not because of the author.

Kevin Rudd is a unique figure. He has studied China, and Chinese, for decades, and dealt with its leaders at the highest level, as a politician, diplomat and scholar. There is really no one else like him. For Rudd, China is a vocation, and his views command attention. So why the scepticism?

Rudd's aim in this book, which is a version of his PhD thesis at Oxford University, is to define Xi Jinping's underlying ideology and elucidate how that has played out in domestic and foreign policy since he came to power in late 2012. Over about 600 pages, a third of which are footnotes, Rudd reconstructs Xi's ideological worldview into a "unifying red thread" illuminating his plans for China and the world.

To do this, like a good PhD student, Rudd eschews amateur psychology and random journalistic excursions and instead sticks painstakingly to Xi's writings and speeches. This is at the heart of Rudd's narrative, as he drives home the need to understand that Xi sees the world through a "historical, cultural and ideational lens" that is profoundly different from that of the West.

Taking Xi at his word is no easy task, as Chinese political discourse is conducted in a kind of linguistic parallel universe to debates in democracies. Political speeches and scholarly articles unfold like dense tracts of the common law, with arcane, codified acknowledgements of precedent ("Mao Zedong Thought", "Deng Xiaoping Theory" and so forth) dutifully piled on top of each other, before a new, incremental judgement is rendered.

Xi is the ultimate activist in this respect. As Rudd shows, Xi has barely given a nod to once-sturdy parts of the communist canon. Rather, he has swept much of it aside to create his own template to allow him to set new rules for governing China. Xi's my-way-or-the-highway approach to governing is couched in the theory of Marxism–Leninism, which has long officially provided the guiding philosophical base for the Chinese Communist Party.

The Leninism part is relatively straightforward. Modern China still runs on Soviet hardware, as designed by Vladmir Lenin, according to which a single ruling party sits above all governing and civil society entities, and both leads and guides them.

The Marxism part is where my scepticism creeps in. To me, the Marxist edifice surrounding Chinese political pronouncements has acted mostly as a form of ideological cladding. In other words, it is an ideology of state power more than a genuine wellspring of governing ideas. Rudd chronicles in minute detail how much Xi disagrees with this assessment. As Xi himself has said, Marx is the "greatest thinker in human history", whose writings "continue to emanate their brilliant rays of truth". In this telling, Marxism is a science that provides the foundation for the immutable laws of history, applied to one's immediate surrounds.

But the process of analysis is one thing. The product of the analysis is another. Deng Xiaoping, for example, proclaimed himself a Marxist and deployed its scientific laws in formulating the rationale to push through a radical change in economic policy in 1978. More than three decades later, Xi used the same foundational ideology to reverse Deng's policy emphasis, this time in favour of the state economy. There's not necessarily a contradiction here, as both leaders simply applied the same toolkit to the circumstances in which they were governing and the direction they thought the country should take.

Rudd convincingly argues that individuals such as Deng and Xi matter in China. They weren't, and aren't, simply "first among equals" in a bland collective leadership. Both Deng and Xi have been brilliant politicians who have been ruthless in bending the vast party apparatus and sprawling bureaucracy – and, by extension, the country – to their will.

But they have diverged significantly as well. As Rudd writes,

Deng thought China laboured under too much politics and theory, and not enough practice and economics. By the time he took over, Xi thought the pendulum had swung too far, so he reversed the formulation. He believed China suffered from too little theory and not enough politics. Accordingly, under Xi, the economy by itself is no longer the number one priority.

But if individuals have agency in the Chinese system, as Deng and Xi did, they also have the ability to manipulate ideological nostrums to get the policy outcome they want. So while Marxism is a permanent fixture of Chinese elite politics, it is also a moving target in the hands of a skilful leader and the band of theoreticians attached to him.

To be fair, Rudd acknowledges this. His focus is overwhelmingly on Xi and his singularity, to the point where he speculates that a successor might depart substantially from the current leader's policies. Of course, any newcomer would have to work over and remake Xi's ideological canon and his version of Marxism to justify any changes.

Rudd is also focused on Xi not just as a Marxist, taking economic policy to the left, but as a nationalist, moving foreign policy to the right. It is a nice formulation.

For readers, there is one caveat about the book, issued by Rudd himself. Put simply, it is a heavy read. Rudd marks out the chapters he thinks are essential, and those where the deep textual analysis might defeat the ordinary reader. His underlying message, and indeed the purpose of the book, is to remind blissed-out Westerners that they won't grasp China, and Xi's import, until they become familiar with its political language, "however stilted and sometimes-unreadable for a Western audience Xi's prose may appear to be. This is something we are all going to have to get used to," Rudd writes.

As a public figure, Rudd has sometimes had to struggle with the absurd notion that just because he has devoted himself to studying China, he is somehow captured by it. In fact, the opposite is usually the case. The more you know about the CCP, the more worried you become about its worldview and ambitions. The same applies to Xi. Understanding Xi and the vast scope of his ambitions is not likely to endear you to him.

Rudd seems to have crossed the Rubicon in his relationship with the CCP with this book. Anything touching Xi is sensitive in China. A thick, unflinching book that cuts to the core of his thinking won't be welcome in Beijing. But, as Rudd writes, "where the CCP is concerned, open and well-reasoned criticism is far better than calculated appeasement".

Amen.

Richard McGregor

Great Game On: The Contest for Central Asia and Global Supremacy
Geoff Raby
Melbourne University Press

Geoff Raby has had a varied career since completing his education at La Trobe University with a PhD in Australian economic history. He spent twenty-seven years in public service with the Department of Foreign Affairs and Trade, including as Australia's ambassador to the World Trade Organization (1998–2001) and to APEC (2003–05). He was based in Beijing from 1986 to 1991 and was Australia's ambassador to China from 2007 to 2011. After 2011 he founded the Beijing-based consulting firm Geoff Raby & Associates. He has published books on Australian economic history, the world trading system and, most recently, China's grand strategy.

That brief bio does little justice to his knowledge of China, which is based not only on his reading and diplomatic career but also on travel. His latest book draws heavily on his travels in 1986–91 and in 2007–11 to the furthest western corners of China and with the Trans-Siberian Railway along the northern side of China's long border with Russia. Before construction of China's high-speed rail system, these travels, lasting many days on hard seats, offered unforgettable insights into China's scale, and the distances involved in the contest between China and Russia for control over Central Asia.

The book's title suggests a symmetry between the 19th-century "Great Game" between Russia and Britain for control over Central Asia and the current contest between China and Russia. The text, however, argues that, despite the popularity of Rudyard Kipling's phrase, the Russian and British empires expanded and edged closer in the late 19th century but avoided conflict by establishing Afghanistan as a buffer. By contrast, the participating countries in the current Great Game between Russia and China are inevitably in competition.

The book's underlying thesis is that in recent decades Russia and China have been drawn together in opposition to the West, but over the long term they have diverse interests, leading to conflict in Central Asia. Russia's role as the dominant power in Central Asia will be challenged by China's desire to establish compliant neighbours outside its distant land borders. Raby expects China to triumph and become the Eurasian superpower.

The book is well-written and the arguments interesting. The combination of personal experience with more conventional history and analysis of international relations makes for some lively anecdotes, but at times the travelogue distracts from the analysis. The reflections Raby makes, while journeying along the Trans-Siberian Railway – on poor Russia–China relations in the Far East and on China's prospects of reclaiming Russia's Far East – end up being too shallow. Similarly, descriptions of trips to Kashgar and to the Central Asian countries are interesting but do not combine easily with analysis of the region's political and economic significance.

The treatment of the five Central Asian countries that became independent in December 1991 is especially disappointing. The book's title suggests it will be about Central Asia, but the Central Asian countries are ignored as independent players in the contest between Russia and China. Differences between Kazakhstan, the Kyrgyz Republic, Tajikistan, Turkmenistan and Uzbekistan, either over the longer term or in the decades since independence, are not discussed. The warning on the third page that Central Asia is now more dangerous than it has been for the last twenty years is not supported by evidence.

Central Asia was under Russian influence from the second half of the

19th century to the dissolution of the USSR in 1991, but there is a story to tell about the five countries' post-1991 attempts to reduce Russia's dominance by improving their relations with other powers. That diplomatic outreach has not meant a simple turn to China, a country treated with suspicion by many in Central Asia. The diminution of the US role in Central Asia after abandoning Afghanistan is rightly emphasised by Raby, but he is silent on the role of the European Union, which is one of the region's three main economic partners. The Duisburg–Chongqing rail link through Kazakhstan – discussed in the book – was at least as much a German initiative as a Chinese one. Raby is silent on middle powers such as Türkiye, Iran, Japan and Korea, which have been active to varying degrees in different Central Asian countries.

Although the background of Russia's role in Central Asia receives early treatment, the historical account is uneven. On page four we read about "centuries" of Russian domination, which is perhaps true if we include the Kazakh steppe, but domination of the Central Asian core only dates from the conquest of Tashkent in 1865.

Dismissing the creation in the 1920s of the Soviet republics that would become nations in 1991 as arbitrary boundary-drawing and imposed Russification is too simplistic. There may have been elements of divide-and-rule, but Joseph Stalin, having witnessed the dissolution of the Austro-Hungarian and Ottoman empires, was aware of the dangers of ethnic nationalism, and the Soviet cartographers tried to match borders with ethnicity. In each republic, national languages continued to be used, and the first secretary was typically from the titular nationality. In the 1989 Soviet census, Kyrgyz, Tajiks, Turkmen and Uzbek were in the majority in their republics, and only Kazakhstan's composition was more complex (two-fifths Kazakh, two-fifths Russian, one-fifth other, largely due to post-1930 migrations). Describing ethnicity as "a bar to an individual's social progress" in the USSR ignores examples such as Stalin, Anastas Mikoyan, Eduard Shevardnadze and many others. This history matters, because today's five Central Asian countries are not arbitrary constructs riven by internal conflict and without national identity, and they are not pawns in a game between Russia and China.

The discussion of Afghanistan, in the chapter "Graveyard of Empires", is good but veers into a political sidetrack with lengthy treatment of Australian reactions to the Soviet invasion of Afghanistan, which seems designed to skewer Malcolm Fraser and to accept Bill Hayden's more benevolent view of the Soviet quest for external stability (eerily similar to Putin's justification for invading Ukraine). The Soviet motivation is not universally agreed, but likely included expanding its sphere of interest and securing access to a year-round ocean port. Australian support for the US invasion of Afghanistan is not discussed. (Incidentally, identifying Afghanistan as the base from which the September 11 attacks was organised seems gratuitous; Hamburg is a better bet.)

The book is a good read, but more care could have been taken with the arguments, as well as with fact-checking. Termez, the entry point for Soviet troops invading Afghanistan, is in Uzbekistan, not Tajikistan. The claim that "the USSR resumed control of all imperial Russian territories" is incorrect: Finland, the Baltic states, eastern Poland and northern Romania were all lost by the Soviet Union and only partially regained in the 1940s. The Shanghai Cooperation Organisation was not "the first formal anti-Western political organization"; predecessors included the Warsaw Pact. Today, moreover, the SCO contains several members that would not generally be considered anti-Western (India, Pakistan) and Dialogue Partners include Saudi Arabia and several gulf states, as well as NATO-member Türkiye.

The book makes many shrewd observations about China and its relations with Russia but some of the assumptions and conclusions are debatable. So far, the two powers have established peaceful cohabitation in Central Asia. The Central Asian countries are not vassals of either power, although they acknowledge the heritage from a century and a half of Russian control and the challenges of maintaining peaceful relations with China. (Notably, none has made official comments on China's treatment of the Uighurs, despite popular sympathy with a fellow Turkic people.) Russia may not like China's increasing presence in Central Asia but is unlikely to adopt a confrontational response. A final observation about great-power competition: despite the subtitle, the book is not about a struggle for global supremacy: that contest must include the United States, which features little in this book.

From his unique vantage point, the author might have provided his views about the implications for Australia of developments in Central Asia. Raby fails to mention Australia's brief foray into a region that would welcome better relations; the embassy in Almaty was closed after four years (1995–99), just before the boom that would transform Kazakhstan. In the 2000s, Australian policy has been based on non-involvement, and trade links have been minor. Areas of potential cooperation include mining, pastoralism, education, Central Asian diasporas and students in Australia, and an export market of 80 million well-educated people in Central Asia: all suggest missed opportunities.

Richard Pomfret

CLIMATE DIPLOMACY

Landing the Paris Agreement: How It Happened, Why It Matters, and What Comes Next
Todd Stern
The MIT Press

For most Australians, mention of the annual United Nations COP climate talks triggers memories of confusing stories about negotiations that had lofty hopes but delivered only incremental progress. These stories are replete with images of bleary-eyed negotiators falling asleep as their deliberations inevitably run into overtime.

In his recently published memoirs, Todd Stern, who was President Obama's climate envoy between the ill-fated Copenhagen summit of 2009 and the securing of the landmark Paris Agreement in 2015, provides a unique insider's perspective on what these negotiations are really like and the meaningful outcomes they can deliver.

Stern, who had previously served in the Clinton White House, was once described by *Rolling Stone* as "a thin, precise man known for his blunt negotiating tactics". His book was released less than a month before

Donald Trump's election to a second term as president, and reading it now is like being transported to a parallel fictional planet where the US government is at the forefront of efforts to rescue humanity from the unfolding climate crisis.

Stern makes digestible the absurdly complex world of climate diplomacy, which he likens to a Bruegel painting. The book has it all: heroes, villains, a failure and then success. Stern brings to life individual diplomats in the manner of a fast-paced thriller rather than a memoir.

(I should note that I have known Stern for over a decade, and worked closely with him during my time as an adviser to Tony deBrum, the late foreign minister of the Marshall Islands, to whom Stern dedicates the book – in part for DeBrum's work in creating the High Ambition Coalition; the HAC helped sow the seeds for success in Paris, which Stern calls the most important agreement this century, and probably for the last century. Stern recalls a French colleague telling him the HAC's final, symbolic march into the plenary "won it". But he deserves credit too, having tried to get a smaller but similar group together, only to yield to the Marshall Islands' initiative, and for helping to publicly raise the need for such a coalition at a critical moment in Paris before the group decided to break cover.)

The story effectively starts with Stern's appointment as Obama's envoy less than a year before the ill-fated Copenhagen talks, where developed and developing countries couldn't agree on a legally binding text. Many of the war stories from that session have already come to light – not least Obama barging in on the Chinese, Indian, Brazilian and South African leaders after Premier Wen Jiabao of China kept evading him. But Stern adds new colour to the pages of history, including how he shouted in desperation at UN Secretary-General Ban Ki-moon for him to change tack when prospects of an outcome were slipping away. (Stern wrote to Ban months later to apologise, but it had the intended effect at the time.)

Stern's book is the kind of fly-on-the-wall stuff that demonstrates that diplomacy is not defined by arcane traditions and protocols, in which diplomats are soulless representatives of their countries. It shows that diplomacy is all about personal relationships, persistence and creativity – and in no arena is that better brought to bear than multilateral negotiations. Stern's account is better than any diplomatic textbook a student could find.

While success always has a thousand parents, Stern is dutiful in dishing out credit where credit is due. He notes the effort of Bo Lidegaard (one of my current bosses) to try to forge a "politically binding" rather than a legally binding outcome in Copenhagen, given that he could see the alternative might be nothing at all. So too Stern's former chief of staff Clare Sierawski's idea for the United States and China to jointly announce their emissions targets in Beijing on 12 November 2014, which was the catalyst for the Paris Agreement, by signalling to the rest of the world that this time there was a deal to be done. Stern mentions DeBrum's idea for countries to set targets every five years, which the United States supported despite the European Union's initial dissent. And he lauds his longstanding professional partner in crime, Sue Biniaz, whose legal wizardry has fixed countless intractable stand-offs. Stern even recalls the idea inspired by his teenage son to visit Brazil for the World Cup and quietly meet with the country's foreign minister when an official visit wasn't politically palatable.

Indeed, one big story Stern tells in parallel is his genuine kinship with his Chinese counterpart, Xie Zhenhua. Stern acknowledges this relationship was kept alive during Trump's last tenure thanks to efforts like one I helped establish with my former boss Kevin Rudd at the Asia Society for backchannel "second track" talks between Democrats like Stern and Chinese figures like Xie. His stories of visiting Xie over the years (who came to call him "his little brother") in his hometown of Tianjin, and of reciprocating by taking Xie to a baseball game in Chicago, illustrate that relationships matter, even when you fervently disagree – as Stern did when he told Xie that China's idea of countries having emissions targets with no process for scrutiny was what Ronald Reagan would have called "trust, but *don't* verify". At one point, Stern intervened to stop a harebrained plan for the White House to go over Xie's head and complain about him, which, if it had happened, could have set history on a very different path.

Australia also gets its fair share of the credit for its creativity along the way. Stern recalls the work Rudd did before Copenhagen to propose that each country set its own target, rather than work from a prescribed collective target, which would have been a non-starter. (Stern says he and the UK's late Pete Betts, to whom he also dedicates the book, also had this idea, calling it "the Agraria model" after the London restaurant where they first discussed it.) He notes Rudd's effort to encourage the establishment of the "Friends of the Chair" group, which effectively crafted the Copenhagen Accord that emerged at the eleventh hour. And he discusses former DFAT official Howard Bamsey's work establishing the Cartagena Dialogue, which helped produce the habits of cooperation between progressive nations in the wake of Copenhagen that ensured they could prevail in Paris.

Stern, a lawyer turned diplomat, is forensic, and I could only find two points of contention in the book's 280 pages. The first is when he includes Australia in the original list of members of the High Ambition Coalition the Marshall Islands helped form in 2015 – despite the then conservative government's creative messaging attempts, this was not the case. And his recollection of when Obama mispronounced Kiribati ("Ki-ri-bas") in a meeting with a handful of island leaders missed the punchline. Stern writes that I-Kiribati president Anote Tong explained that there is no letter "i" in their language. DeBrum, with his cheeky exuberance, proclaimed to the room that it must have been American missionaries who stole it.

Stern does not dwell at length on the possibility of another Trump victory. But he suggests the US Climate Alliance – a bipartisan group of twenty-five state governors – could appoint their own shadow envoy. Nevertheless, the entire international climate regime has been effectively negotiated for the last thirty years on the basis of the limitations of the US body politic (or, more specifically, the US Senate) – a constraint that is a clear backdrop of Stern's book. That is as much a story about diplomatic pragmatism as it is about US exceptionalism, but it underscores the danger of Trump withdrawing not only from the Paris Agreement again (as he has now begun) but also, in the future, from the underlying framework convention too. This would be diabolical but also legally contestable as to the limits of executive authority, given the United States' accession was ratified by the Senate – something that was possible in the Republican Party of George H.W. Bush but is not in the Republican Party of today, or likely for several electoral cycles to come. Stern recalls how even the fact that 2015 became the critical deadline for an agreement to be forged (rather than 2016) was at the European Union's behest, for fear of what would happen if the Democrats lost the presidential race.

With Australia bidding to host the COP31 Climate Conference in 2026, Stern's book is a masterclass for Australia's officials if they are to embark on what would be the biggest diplomatic gathering we have ever held, with potentially a hundred world leaders and tens of thousands of delegates. More importantly, it would be an opportunity for us – irrespective of Trump – to accelerate our own transition towards clean energy and a decarbonised trade balance sheet.

Thom Woodroofe

Correspondence

"Fateful mix: Great powers, strongman leaders and manifest destinies" by Michael Wesley

Benjamin Moffitt

In "Fateful Mix" (Australian Foreign Affairs 22), Michael Wesley describes the situation that confronts the international order today: things are changing, and fast. He notes that we are facing not only a shift from unipolarity to tripolarity but a trend "that has emerged in the international arena over the past two decades, which has seen a different type of leader rise to power". These figures, whom he calls "strongman leaders", are charismatic, see their personal destiny and the destiny of the nation as intertwined, and tend to become the dominant figures in their countries' political landscapes. Moreover, these strongman leaders are currently in charge of the four countries central to Australia's future: India, China, Indonesia and the United States.

I share many of Wesley's concerns but I think his diagnosis of the problem is incorrect. First, he overplays the charisma card. Second, his argument is somewhat ahistorical, exoticising a form a leadership as somehow "new" that has actually been around for a very long time. In doing so, he falls into some of the old-fashioned thinking that he otherwise rightly calls for us to move past.

First, charisma. The thrust of Wesley's argument is this: the problem we are dealing with is not just that these strongmen are bad news for democracy, it's that they are charismatic. This makes them different to what he calls "conventional leaders". Putting aside the question of whether the leaders he talks about are indeed charismatic – I have my doubts about the charisma of Xi Jinping, for instance, and whether such a "charismatic" leader would have to resort to increasingly repressive behaviour – I think the claim is overplayed, as is the novelty of charisma in the current context.

In an era of celebritised and mediatised politics, charisma is part and parcel of political leadership. It is not just the domain of dangerous strongmen. Indeed, Barack Obama has arguably been the most charismatic politician of the 21st century, and we do not tend to associate his leadership with democratic decay. Exoticising charisma as a shady technique of autocrats does us no favours.

Moreover, charisma has its limits in the shifting media landscape. As Julia Sonnevend's excellent book *Charm: How Magnetic Personalities Shape Global Politics* argues, we increasingly want leaders who can tap into the idea that they are "just like us" and who project intimacy in an age of social media. This is charm rather than charisma – leaders who take us into their personal lives and seek to perform authenticity, rather than larger-than-life bombast. It is something the likes of Modi, with his narrative of "just" being a humble tea seller, has excelled at – he is a charmer with all the tools of digital technology available to him, rather than a charismatic firebrand.

Second, Wesley's argument is ahistorical. He writes: "Modern politics is being transformed by the discovery of the power of emotions. Evoking fear, contempt, hope or anger is increasingly more effective than appeals to rationality, self-interest or the public good." The "discovery" of the power of emotions? This would be news to Aristotle, Plato, Hobbes and Hume, who all wrote about the relationship between emotions and politics. Emotions are – and have always been – at the core of politics; what else can explain the attachment of people to their national communities, the bond they feel with leaders or the passions that stir them to try to change the world? And why are emotions necessarily dangerous? To return to the example of Obama, the positive emotion of "hope" was the central motif of his presidency. All leaders play on emotions, not just "charismatic strongmen". Beyond this, setting up a binary between emotions (read: bad) and "rationality, self-interest or the public good" (read: good) perpetuates an outdated notion of the citizen as *Homo politicus* who rationally does a cost-benefit analysis when considering who to vote for. It's simply not how politics works.

Wesley is right to call for a more nuanced understanding of what Australia will face strategically in the coming decades, but I fear he doesn't go far enough in moving beyond the binaries of the past that his argument clings to:

charismatic versus "conventional" leaders, emotional versus rational politics, and even "normal" versus not-so-normal politics. We are in a moment of flux, not just in our diplomatic relations, but in what political leadership looks like today.

As such, it's not charisma that is the problem here, nor the "discovery" of the power of emotions in politics. If these leaders were charismatic champions of the liberal order who used emotional appeals to defend it, we wouldn't be having this discussion. The issue is that these figures are radically illiberal, and that they are rapidly gaining ground as the liberal world order is under threat. Moving past these binaries will be vital if we are to navigate and survive the years to come.

Benjamin Moffitt is senior lecturer in politics & international relations at Monash University, and the author of several books on populism around the globe.

Asha Clementi

Michael Wesley has deftly explained the playbook of the world's strongmen, and, in the coming decade, it is something we will have to pay attention to. Australia will have a delicate tightrope to walk while balancing the egos of these great powers' leaders, and President Trump's re-election only adds to the strongman trifecta of Xi Jinping in China, Narendra Modi in India and Prabowo Subianto in Indonesia. There is almost a guarantee that the next four years will be defined by a whirlwind of strong tempers, major announcements breaking on podcasts and a cut-throat social media cycle.

It will be all too easy, within this ego-defined era, for Australia to lose sight of its strategic priorities. Wesley's and Malcolm Turnbull's calls for a "reformulation of Australian statecraft" in response to these leaders is necessary – Australia must define its own values and stick to them. In defining our values, policymakers must consider all Australians, not just those in the Canberra bubble. The perspectives of rural Australians, minorities, women and others must be actively considered in the shaping of our foreign policy. As these authoritarian leaders rise around us, the role of the public in politics has never been more crucial. Political participation will be the key to ensuring these leaders are held to high standards. Accountability will be crucial to maintaining our values of democracy and equality when they waver elsewhere in the world.

Historically, the presence of strongmen leaders has meant the erosion of gender equality, women's rights and human rights more broadly. We are already seeing the influence of the 2024 US presidential election on our shores, with renewed discussion of limiting sexual and reproductive rights. As Australia looks to define its values, we must be wary of these influences and how much we give up in order to appeal to these strongman leaders. While Wesley has outlined what makes strongman leaders successful in their own countries, Turnbull's expansion on how to deal with them should be equally weighted. What neither of them apply, however, is a gendered analysis.

This prediction of the strongmen-led tripolar order in Asia is almost defined by a lack of female presence. We see three great powers – the United States, China and India – led by men with autocratic tendencies and who are served by male foreign ministers. These leaders, particularly in the United States and Indonesia, have been domestically elected with a swell of support from young men, a demographic that is increasingly showing a concerning trend towards believing that gender equality has gone too far.

For me, this raises a number of questions. How might Australia view its position differently if even one of those leadership roles were held by a woman? What will be the effect of our own foreign minister, Penny Wong, being an openly gay woman? And how will we define our values in the face of these increasingly illiberal friends?

The issues that have led to this strongman-dominated global order will not go away anytime soon. The increased cost of living and the decline of material conditions, particularly among young people, means that, as Wesley identified, many are looking for someone to save them. These strongmen present saviour narratives that are often used to create division and prey on high-emotion issues with simple, quick-fix solutions, often with a throwback to outdated-for-a-reason traditions. Australia may find that these solutions lead to a clash of values with some of its most important partners – a situation I think we need to prepare for.

As a young woman, I am anxious to see which values Australia sticks to and which it allows to be swept under the rug. Timidity is not an option when human rights are at stake, though that seems to be forgotten when convenient. It may be too much to ask that Australia face up to these great-power egos over challenges like human rights and climate change, but I hope we will work to establish a place in this emerging global order that sees us push for progress.

As Wesley says, we "must anticipate the fallout and be ready to adapt". This adaptation will require us to be ready for all scenarios and to be solid in our stances. The next question is: how much will we allow those stances to be influenced by our great-power "friends"?

Asha Clementi is the founder and CEO of Girls Run the World, and leads the Women in Strategic Policy program in collaboration with the Strategic and Defence Studies Centre at ANU.

Michael Wesley responds

Australian foreign policy has been lucky for decades that the United States, China, India and Indonesia have been led by cautious, conventional leaders who have sent few surprises our – and the world's – way. Now, following the election of Donald Trump, we have the quadfecta – ego-driven, hypernationalist, unpredictable leaders heading the nations that comprise our four most consequential bilateral relationships. The next four years and beyond will be a wild ride, and we need to get ready for it.

Benjamin Moffitt disagrees with my diagnosis of the problem but, somehow, agrees with my conclusions. He disagrees with my labelling these leaders "charismatic", interpreting this in the conventional meaning of the word (charming, persuasive, magnetic, good-looking – he raises the case of Barack Obama), despite my clearly stating that this is not the sense of the word I am using. I used a specific sense of the term, as written about by Max Weber a century ago, which describes a particular relationship between such a leader and his followers, as well as the particular calling and self-belief of such a leader.

This is no mere semantic quibble. It is important to the second part of "Fateful Mix" because my argument is that a particular emotional attachment between leader and followers, and a particular sense of calling and self-belief, has profound effects when that leader is in command of a great power. Trump's claims to Greenland and the Panama Canal speak to a geopolitical posturing with an eye to keeping his base energised that simply would not work for the leader of a less powerful country – and would not have been considered by any of his predecessors. Trump appears to believe that just as he is not constrained by the conventions of domestic politics, so the country he leads (while he's commander-in-chief) is unconstrained by the conventions of international relations. It is an unhinged form of exceptionalism.

Moffitt's second objection is that I am being ahistorical in claiming modern politics is being transformed by the power of emotions, referencing Aristotle, Plato, Hobbes and Hume. He is right in observing that emotion has long been a part of politics, though I'm not sure "all" leaders play on emotions – he must have missed John Major's soporific premiership. What I'm careful to argue in "Fateful Mix" is that contemporary politics has at its disposal a range of new technologies – from social media to behavioural psychology – that enables the injection of increasing levels of emotion into politics, and to maintain a state of constant activation among supporters. To deny there's something different in today's technology-enabled politics of emotion compared to previous eras strikes me as its own form of ahistoricism.

Asha Clementi raises an interesting question: would a woman leader consider a charismatic strategy, and would she be successful if so? There are certainly strong elements of gender in the character of a charismatic leader – the focus on virility and masculinity, the overweening self-belief, the determination to belittle opponents – that suggest it is a route only open to men. We are yet to see a female equivalent of a Trump, Erdoğan or Duterte.

Clementi observes that the rise of such leaders invariably leads to the erosion of the rights of and respect for women in their societies. This raises the intriguing possibility that the rise of charismatic male leaders is particularly possible during times of social backlash against what are perceived as the exaggerated advances of progressive agendas. She raises the dilemma now facing Trump's opponents: how do they oppose all that he stands for without further provoking the forces that returned him to the White House?

The challenge, as Clementi writes, will be how Australia should "play" this new type of leadership in such crucial countries. In the short term, Australia, like pretty much every other country, will have to be attentive to the ego and the unpredictability, using every interest and advantage wisely. But there is a longer-term question: if great powers are prone to producing such leaders, how should we position ourselves vis-à-vis these four large powers that are so crucial to us? Surely this should provoke a profound reconsideration of the bases and frameworks of Australian foreign policy.

Michael Wesley is deputy vice chancellor (Global, Culture and Engagement) and professor of politics at the University of Melbourne.

The Back Page

FOREIGN POLICY CONCEPTS AND JARGON, EXPLAINED

REGLOBALISATION

What is it: Reglobalisation typically refers to a more equitable version of globalisation, in which countries diversify their economies by finding a wider range of partners. Matthew Bishop and Anthony Payne (academics, Sheffield University) describe it as "re-doing globalization better".

Who coined it: The term originally referred to the post–World War II trading era, but a new usage emerged in response to the era of rising protectionism. Roland Benedikter (political scientist, Eurac Research) says reglobalisation marks a "renewal of the neoliberal-hyper-cosmopolitan era that lasted from the end of the 1980s until the mid-2010s".

Top reglobaliser: Ngozi Okonjo-Iweala (director-general, World Trade Organization) has championed reglobalisation as a way of promoting trade with lower-income countries and potential manufacturing hubs such as Mexico, Vietnam and Cambodia. She told *The Washington Post* that such countries "normally don't benefit from the global supply chain and could be brought in".

Offshoots: Other experts have argued that globalisation is slowing (known as "slowbalisation"), or fracturing ("localisation"), or reversing ("deglobalisation"). Sebastian Franco-Bedoya (economist, World Bank) says the competing terms all tell "a very different story about changes in the world economy", though he insists that one of these stories – deglobalisation – is wrong.

Final word: Braz Baracuhy (diplomat, Brazil) has argued that the main reason globalisation is evolving is the rivalry between the United States and China. In January, before the World Economic Forum meeting at Davos, he unveiled his own term to describe this phenomenon: "bi-globalisation".